Coaching, Learning, and Action

by Bill C. Lovin
and Emery Reber Casstevens

Illustrated by Al Hormel

American Management Association, Inc.

International standard book number: 0-8144-5249-3
Library of Congress catalog card number: 70-138568

FIRST PRINTING

Preface

THIS book is intended as a practical aid for people who do on-the-job coaching. They may have a variety of titles—supervisors, superintendents, hospital administrators, department heads, sales managers, district managers, general foremen, foremen—or they may have no titles at all. If you are a serious practitioner of on-the-job coaching or even just a student of its skills, this book is for you. Its purpose is to show you how to get better results from coaching. It is meant to be both a useful tool and an aid to understanding the various processes that make up the practice of coaching. It shows alternative strategies, methods, techniques, and devices for coaching so that these fundamentals can be easily understood and effective choices made.

The book can be used as a primary text for training sessions on coaching in industry, service organizations, governmental agencies, hospitals, and sales organizations. It can also be used as supplementary reading material for college classes in organizational behavior, personnel management, leadership, teacher training, and supervisory practices. Containing, as it does, a description of each of the most commonly used techniques and devices of coaching, it can also be used as a handbook or reference book. Portions of it, for example, might be read before an appraisal interview or a joint-planning conference. The result should be a more profitable interview through a keener awareness of the purposes and procedures of the entire coaching process.

For nearly all of our adult lives we, the authors, have been primarily responsible for changing the habitual behavior of adults on the job. For the past decade we have concentrated on helping supervisors learn how to coach their subordinates on the job. We are grateful to each of these supervisors for adding his own unique contribution to our insight and for the color and flavor of the examples used. Many of them will recognize these examples, though we hope we have disguised them sufficiently. In only two or three instances have we synthesized. The other examples are events that have actually happened.

We also acknowledge here our appreciation to our associates at Southern Illinois University, Edwardsville, Ill., and Mercantile Trust Company.

Bill C. Lovin
Emery Reber Casstevens

Contents

1   Introduction   1
      The Supervisor-Subordinate
         Relationship / *4*

2   Understanding Adult Learning   20
      Definition of Adult Learning / *21*
      Obstacles to Adult Learning / *22*

3   How Adults Learn   28
      The Nonthreatening Approach / *28*
      Learning from the Environment / *33*
      The Four-Step Process / *34*
      Self-Actualization / *38*

4   Distinctive Characteristics of
         Adult Learning   43
      Two Powerful Influences / *44*
      Skills Are Learned by Doing / *51*

5   The Framework of Coaching   58
     What Is On-the-Job Coaching / 59
     What Can Coaching Do? / 61
     What Is the Role of the Coach? / 64
     What Devices Can the Coach Use? / 69

6   Three Coaching Strategies   79
     Change the Environment / 81
     Use Reward and Punishment / 85
     Supervise Key Points / 92

7   Three More Coaching Strategies   99
     Encourage Joint Planning / 100
     Control the Rate a Subordinate
          Takes on Responsibility / 105
     Concentrate on Strengths and
          Weaknesses / 110

8   Specific Coaching Situations   118
     Coaching's Common
          Denominators / 119
     Cases / 129
     Coaching in Special Situations / 141

9   Dealing with Difficult Employee
          Behavior   145

10   A Final Review of Coaching   158

     Annotated Bibliography   164

1

Introduction

"A MAN'S development is 90 percent the result of his experience in his day-to-day work." Research headed by General Electric's Moorhead Wright yielded this conclusion in the late 1950s. "Outside interviewers asked 300 top General Electric managers, 'What was most important to your development?' Ninety percent replied, 'It was working for so-and-so at such-and-such a place.' Only 10 percent gave credit to such other factors as educational background, special courses, or rotation." [1] These man-

[1] "Help Yourself to Executive Skill," *Nation's Business,* Vol. 46, No. 9 (September 1958), pp. 68–72.

1

agers grew because they had bosses who helped them, who taught them. Their bosses were coaches.

This research at General Electric is one of the early developments that started the ground swell of recent interest in on-the-job coaching. This growing interest, fed by research findings and supported by the experience of many companies, suggests that what a person learns on the job is vital to his own progress and to the progress of his organization.

Executives have accepted the fact that they must help their people learn. But many executives do not know how to help. For one thing, their businesses and their staffs change rapidly, so, as the executives try to direct their attention to the techniques, devices, and approaches used in coaching, they are faced with a shifting target. Another reason coaching is generally not good is that the coaches have simply not thought enough about it. They feel the need to coach more and better, but many have not worked out how to do it. The principles, if there are any, have not been identified and widely studied. Yet there is hardly anything that a coach could do that would yield more results than identify and study the *principles* of coaching.

The principles followed by a coach, consciously or unconsciously, are directly related to his ideas about why people work and what makes them work better. Douglas McGregor has suggested that a person's managerial style is determined by the assumptions he makes about people's attitudes toward work.[2] Since his managerial responsibilities include coaching, these same assumptions affect his coaching style—how he selects and applies coaching techniques, devices, and strategies.

McGregor has identified two managerial theories which he calls Theory X and Theory Y. Theory X assumes that the average person dislikes work, must be coerced to work, and wishes to avoid responsibility. Theory Y assumes that work is natural, that the average person will work hard for objectives of his own choosing, and that he seeks responsibility. These two theories have been the subject of a great deal of study, and it is apparent that most people prefer to believe Theory Y.

These concepts may lead the practitioner of on-the-job coaching to a better understanding of the kind of attitude that workers respond to. The coach should be aware of these concepts so that he can use them as the foundation for his study of the broad subject of individual employee development. The growth of people, like the growth of plants, is strongly influenced by environment. A plant's growth depends on how favorable and stimulating the climate is, the richness of the soil, and the nature of its cultivation. A person's growth depends on the extent to which favorable and stimulating attitudes are present in the

[2] Douglas McGregor, *The Human Side of Enterprise* (New York: McGraw-Hill Book Co., Inc., 1960), pp. 33–57.

workplace; the richness of the knowledge, abilities, and understanding of his coach; and the nature of the experiences he is exposed to. As the gardener must plan and work to provide the optimum conditions for his plants to grow strong, so the coach must plan and work to provide the optimum conditions to enable his subordinates to grow strong. This is what we mean by coaching—the supervisor's job of providing the conditions that will cause the people under his direction to grow and develop.

THE SUPERVISOR-SUBORDINATE RELATIONSHIP

A major and basic part of the conditions in which growth takes place is the supervisor-subordinate relationship itself. The primary on-the-job influence on the subordinate is the supervisor, whose attitude is a matter of critical concern to the employee. The working relationship between them forms the basis for the communication essential both to job effectiveness and to individual development. Here is an example of how a person may feel on a new job:

Monday morning, when Frank Johnson reported to his new job in the stamping department, everything seemed strange. He was especially aware of the noise, a rhythmic pounding that he found vaguely disturbing. He supposed that he would get used to it eventually. The place seemed crowded

*The coach must plan and work
to provide the optimum conditions
to enable his subordinates to grow strong.*

with people when he compared it with the shipping department, where he had worked until last Friday. Frank had requested the transfer, but, now that he was actually assigned to the new department, he was beginning to have doubts. He had not realized how few people in the stamping department he had even seen before. As he looked around, he didn't see one familiar face. A forklift went by and for a moment Frank felt like running up and saying "Hi!" He then looked around self-consciously to see if the other men were aware of his silly impulse.

As he approached the office of his new supervisor, Joe Korlak, he saw that he would have to wait because Joe was busy. He wondered what kind of fellow Joe really was. Joe

5

had interviewed him before the transfer and had seemed friendly enough. But interviewing a man is not the same as working for him. How friendly would Joe be if, for example, he were three men short, or if he had a machine breakdown and had just been chewed out because an order was behind schedule? Well, he would find out soon enough. As he waited, Frank felt excited, tense, and a little apprehensive.

When a person reports to a new job, he may be filled more with apprehension than with eager expectation. He would like to find a few familiar things—a machine he has used before, a system he has some knowledge of, duties he has performed successfully in other situations. He may regard these impersonal things as old friends, and he has the need to relate to something familiar.

As he settles into his new job, he will form new personal relationships. Some will be casual or relatively insignificant; others will be important, as he establishes himself in the social structure of the organization. The most important relationship of all will be his relationship with his boss. This will influence his feelings toward his work, toward his work group, and toward the total organization far more than any other single affiliation. How he regards himself and his value to the organization will depend in large part on how his supervisor regards him.

The subordinate's view of his supervisor is as important as his view of himself. The subordinate may see his supervisor as a substitute father without the other's knowledge or consent and may maintain this image in spite of the supervisor's vigorous attempts to dislodge it. A person may regard his supervisor, either overtly or covertly, as an authoritarian figure or even as an opponent. He may force these and other roles upon his supervisor because of something deep in his past over which neither he nor his supervisor has much control.

It is evident that when the supervisor attempts to influence the behavior of an employee, he must do this within the framework of their relationship. This is why a supervisor must be judicious in selecting the coaching techniques he wants. What worked for Frank in the shipping department may not work at all for Charley in accounts receivable. If you are a father image to Jane, a boss-on-a-pedestal to Joe, and the personification of the injustice of the "system" to Pete, you cannot expect identical results if you use similar coaching techniques with each. Treating everybody alike would not only be impractical, it would be impossible.

A powerful factor influencing the nature of the supervisor-subordinate relationship is ambition. Consider the young college graduate. He has untried abilities that demand to be tested; he is hungry for the satisfaction of a job well done; he needs proof of his ability to succeed in the competitive world of business. Compare him with an older man whose seniority as a craftsman and whose high degree of skill have placed him at the top of the merit-rating scale. This man's only chance for advancement would be into a supervisory position which he may or may not want and which he may or may not be qualified for. Both these men need a supervisor, but for distinctly different reasons. It is logical, then, to assume that the relationships these men have with their supervisors would contrast sharply.

Ambition makes some people eager to please, solicitous, and willing to do anything no matter how unreasonable as long as they do not risk the displeasure of the boss. In others, a lack of ambition (at least as it shows itself in a desire for a higher-rated job) causes them to not want the extra responsibility inherent in a promotion. This lack of ambition may even cause them to behave in such a way that they are assured of not being promoted. Few factors are more important to coaching than the nature and intensity of a subordinate's ambition, for these will determine the kind of stimuli to which he will respond. His personal goals, what is important to him, what he wants for himself—these are the factors that feed his enthusiasm and that form the basis for his interaction with others.

The process of forming and maintaining a pattern of interaction between a supervisor and an employee may be thought of as a continuing negotiation. In abbreviated form, it is similar to the negotiation between union and management when they declare positions, define attitudes, communicate expectations, make demands and counterdemands, hint at possible concessions, discuss conditions for compromise, trade point for point, and finally work out the rules and understandings under which they agree to operate. Two people follow the same process in creating a working relationship.

Each person establishes his negotiating demands. Each must decide how much power he will be content with. He alone must determine how much approval of his work he needs. He must decide to what extent he requires respect for his abilities and he must decide to what extent he will allow himself to depend on others. But the other fellow has demands and conditions too, and so, during the negotiating process, there is a contest, but there is also cooperation. These two conditions coexist because the two persons need each other. Thus compromises must be made. Results are measured and positions adjusted. The negotiations go on continuously. Ultimately a unique mixture of trust, openness, respect, and approval, and their opposites will be worked out. Shifting conditions, however, will demand that the relationship be fluid and that negotiations not cease but continue to some extent for as long as the relationship exists.

Verticalness Versus Horizontalness

A supervisor-subordinate relationship is shaped to a significant degree by the relative emphasis each places on verticalness and horizontalness. Verticalness refers to those factors in a relationship which

A supervisor-subordinate relationship is shaped by the relative emphasis each places on verticalness and horizontalness.

tend to emphasize that the two people are on different organizational levels. Horizontalness implies the equality of all men regardless of position, rank, or social level. The concept of verticalness is built into practically every organization. An organization has a head or a leader who has authority, responsibilities, and privileges that others do not have. He is said to be "over" the rest of the organization. He may even refer to it as "his" organization, and to the people in it as his people. Others who work for the same organization are called subordinates and they are said to work "under" the boss.

This verticalness concept attempts to represent reality in simplified form. It endures because it is useful. However, the horizontalness concept is also useful. It represents people as having equal worth but different functions. Each job performed in an organization is presumed to be necessary. If it were not, it would be eliminated. But, aside from their function, all people are considered to be equally deserving of respect and consideration.

A man and his boss influence their relationship by the relative stress they place on verticalness and horizontalness. Consider the case of Jim Davis who was transferred to the department headed by Norman Johnson:

About three years before the transfer, Jim and Norman had discovered that they had a mutual friend in the company where Jim had worked previously. Jim and Norman had coffee together and conversed comfortably about all manner of subjects which branched out from the mention of a mutual friend. Soon a casual, relaxed horizontal relationship was established between them. They were not especially close, but, if they met in the hall or the lunchroom, they would exchange some kind of banter or casual grapevine gossip. Then Jim was transferred to Norman's department.

Norman immediately requested that Jim report to his office. He stated what he wanted Jim to do, how he wanted it done, what reports would be required, and when—the whole job. It wasn't so much what he said as how he said it that made Jim feel that their previous horizontal relationship was gone.

The boss knew what he wanted and it was clear that he expected Jim to do it. Jim knew that Norman had a right to do this. However, he felt that in the future he could not speak as freely and as openly as he had in the past. He felt that he would have to think a while before speaking, try to guess how Norman would react, and say only what he thought would bring a favorable reaction. Thus Jim had set up a filter in his mind and Norman would never have access to all Jim's thoughts. He would get only what Jim was willing to give him. Hence, conversations between Norman and Jim were more like a game than a frank exchange. And this was the time when both men most needed full and open communication.

Thus we see how a congenial horizontal relationship changed into a not so congenial vertical relationship where communications were blocked. Any experienced supervisor has seen this happen when he was assigned a new man whom he had previously known personally. This example, seen from Jim's point of view, illustrates how the change from horizontalness to verticalness can lessen rapport and block honest communication.

There are very few companies that have attempted to eliminate some of the symbols that advertise the vertical nature of the supervisor-subordinate relationship. They have tried to eliminate not the status of the supervisor, but the status symbols; not the authority of the supervisor, but the authority symbols. It is still true in most organizations, however, that square feet of office space is a reliable measure of rank. The presence or absence of a carpet is a sure indicator of status as is a reserved parking space, a carafe and water glass on the desk, a private dining room, and dozens of other items.

Sometimes symbols are reliable indicators of the true attitudes of the people who display them, and these symbols are important only because they seem to reveal attitudes so accurately. The supervisor's job of providing conditions for growth can be made more difficult by these symbols if his employees conclude from them that their boss is so remote that a person-to-person relationship is not possible.

The Supervisor as Teacher

We have seen that the supervisor's attitudes play a dominant role in setting the tone for negotiation in the supervisor-subordinate relationship and in de-termining the balance between horizontalness and verticalness. Because of this dominant role, the super-visor is in a position to greatly influence a subordi-nate's learning process. However, the supervisor may not be as aware of this as his subordinate is. In fact, there is evidence that the supervisor's influence on the subordinate's learning is one of the primary fac-tors in the subordinate's evaluation of his boss. You can verify this by asking several people, "Who was the best boss you ever had?" And then ask for a brief description of this boss. After many people have been asked, you can discern a definite pattern in the responses. The best boss is the one under whose direction the person learned the most and expe-rienced the most personal growth. Thus the boss is evaluated in terms of the personal interests and the long-term objectives of the evaluator. In other words, "What has this person done for me?" or "What can he do for me?" Since we all tend to see the world in terms of our own interests, it is not sur-prising that we rate our supervisors in terms of their contribution to our own growth. Although a super-visor may not have anticipated his role as a trainer or a teacher, he must perform it because it is a vital part of the supervisor-subordinate relationship.

Many years ago it was common practice in the highly skilled trades for young men to be appren-tices of a single master craftsman. Men who learned a trade under this system speak of it with such a mixture of nostalgia and pride that it makes us wonder if some magic was used. It is common to hear a former apprentice boast of how tough his master-teacher was, how high his standards were, how intolerant he was of sloppy work, how rigid a disciplinarian he was—not only of his pupil but of himself. What was there about this relationship which evokes, so many years later, this sentimental pride?

Hero worship is always an element in any good teacher-pupil relationship. The pupil adopts the teacher as his model, attributing to him all the virtues and none of the faults of other men. He is an example to be emulated, a guide to be followed. This may be due in part to the master's role as a teacher. There was discipline in this affiliation and a certain harshness tempered with concern for the pupil. The master insisted on high standards but gave willing and skillful guidance to help the apprentice attain these standards. And he set an example. Intolerance of mistakes created tension, but this was counteracted by the protection from outside interference. The apprentice understood that he must be responsible for his work or suffer the consequences, but he also had the assurance that the consequences, though immediate and severe, would be confined to the job situation. The possibility that he might fail to please the master was present, but he would not embarrass both himself and the master by sending out uninspected, inferior work.

An understanding of the master-apprentice relationship is helpful to the understanding of the supervisor-subordinate relationship. Eileen Thompson, nursing instructor at Memorial Hospital, applied some of the principles of the old master-apprentice arrangement in the training of young student nurses.

Eileen was fair but firm, and the young students knew that she would stand for no monkey business. Sometimes they were vexed by her methods. Karen Holden, in particular, thought it was senseless to spend so much time on the same tiresome routines.

One day Karen ventured a comment: "Miss Thompson, I hope you don't think I'm impertinent, but for a whole week now you've had us sticking needles in oranges. I just don't understand why it is necessary to do this over and over again. I know that giving injections takes technique, but I feel kind of silly doing this so much."

Miss Thompson stopped, glared, and said, "All right, let's see your technique. Here's an orange. Imagine that it is a sick and very tender patient." Karen demonstrated. Miss Thompson stopped her. "Not that way. Here, let me show you. Now watch the angle, speed, and pressure carefully." Miss Thompson "shot" the orange with all the accumulated art and skill of a couple of dozen years. "Now you try it and keep on trying until you can do it as well as I can. Next week you girls are going to start practicing on each other. You're lucky you don't have to practice on yourself. You have all the skill of a bear wearing mittens."

It wasn't easy, but Karen learned. And she noticed that the older nurses who had trained under Miss Thompson commanded considerable respect. She heard them say that you could spot a Thompson-trained nurse within five minutes.

As Miss Thompson illustrates, some of the master-apprentice techniques are still being applied effectively on modern-day jobs. However, the tension created by intolerance of mistakes has come under question in recent years.

Important research involving tension in on-the-job learning was done by Dr. M. Scott Myers and Earl R. Gomersall of Texas Instruments, Inc.[3] These men had at one time observed that, in breaking in new operators on industrial jobs, productivity was low at first and tension was high. Tension decreased as the person learned the job, so that by the time productivity had risen to acceptable standards, tension had been reduced to tolerable levels. It was, therefore, assumed that tension existed *because* productivity was low. But this new research offers strong evidence that the reverse is true: Productivity was low because tension was high.

Myers and Gomersall set up a procedure aimed at reducing tension among newly hired operators at the earliest possible time. They arranged for the trainees to become acquainted with the job and its surroundings, and with the supervisor, before performing any productive work. They found that this reduced the tension; hence learning took place more rapidly and productivity quickly rose to acceptable

[3] Earl R. Gomersall and M. Scott Myers, "Breakthrough in On-the-Job Training," *Harvard Business Review,* Vol. 44, No. 4 (July–August 1966), pp. 62–72.

levels. Not only did they find that productivity could be influenced by tension, but they also found that productivity rose past the acceptable level to the mastery level in a shorter period of time.

Another thing they discovered was that one of the primary causes for tension was apprehension over what kind of person the supervisor would be. This suggests that the supervisor-subordinate relationship not only affects the learning curve but it affects the productivity level as well. It also makes a strong case for the early reduction of job tension and for horizontal relationships. At the same time, it does nothing to suggest that the high standards of the master-apprentice arrangement are inappropriate. It does favor a shift from emphasizing the dire consequences of mistakes to providing the help necessary to achieve high standards.

The supervisor-subordinate relationship, in summary, is a highly complex, important factor in the overall effectiveness of an organization. It is also an important element in the development of people who work in an organization. It may be vertically or horizontally oriented or some combination of the two. The relationship is powerfully affected by the expectations of the two persons involved, as well as by their ambitions. We have seen that the supervisor's role as teacher and the subordinate's role as learner make up a major portion of the total relationship. The development of the employee on the job takes place within this relationship; mistakes are made and dealt with, coaching techniques are applied, and a person grows or fails to grow within the limits of this complex social structure.

2

Understanding Adult Learning

THE job provides the locale for adult learning, and the supervisor-subordinate relationship provides the climate. The combination of climate and locale comprises the social structure of the workplace within which job-related adult learning occurs. But how does this learning take place? And, what are adults willing to learn? When will they learn, and why? Learning is, of course, many-sided and can be understood, and even then imperfectly, only by considering what, when, where, why, and how.

DEFINITION OF ADULT LEARNING

A definition of learning is a prerequisite to understanding how learning occurs. How can we know whether someone learns or not unless we establish what learning is? If a man repeats from memory the steps in the operation of a drill press and then, when he's on the job, he omits the third step, thereby ruining an expensive part, can we say that he has learned? If a route salesman, at a company training conference, is taught to explain to customers how his company's customer service is superior to that of his competitors and then fails to mention service on a sales visit, can we say that he has learned? Or, if a supervisor reads a book on McGregor's Theory X and Theory Y and decides that Theory Y would yield better results but continues the practices of Theory X, has he learned? Two technicians attend a night school course on laboratory practices. One receives a grade of A, the other a B. Did the former learn more than the latter? Did either learn anything? How can we know what learning is, and how can we measure it? Obviously, we need a definition.

There are many ideas about what constitutes learning. One is that *learning is a modification of behavior through experience.* This best defines adult

21

learning because it includes action, and adult learning is action-oriented. (Learning when related to children may need a different definition.) In regard to the preceding questions, a drill press operator who can tell you the third step in the operation of his machine but fails to use this step has not learned. Nor has the salesman who understands the importance of customer service well enough to explain it, but who fails to stress it in his sales effort. Their learning is incomplete because they have not reached the final step in the learning process, which is action. The following maxim expresses the concept of learning as it is used in our discussion:

> *To look is one thing.*
> *To see what you look at is another.*
> *To understand what you see is a third.*
> *To learn from what you understand is still something else.*
> *To act on what you learn is all that really matters.*

The person who acts habitually, consistently, and effectively on what he learns has fulfilled the requirements of the definition; he has modified his behavior through experience.

OBSTACLES TO ADULT LEARNING

Just as habitual behavior must sometimes be changed, so must habitual ways of thinking. One of the strongest enemies to adult learning is the half-truth that has become accepted. We often assume that concepts that are stated concisely and that have lasted a long time must be true. The adage "Experience is the best teacher" is an example. It is an old accepted idea, but, in reality, it is only a half-truth. In fact, a person does learn from experience, but a person who has worked in an organization for twenty years is not necessarily better qualified to make decisions concerning it than a person who has been with that organization one year. Furthermore, when this maxim is quoted as proof that a person with many years on a job has learned it and therefore need learn no more, it is being used as a shield to protect its user from the pain of learning. When it is used to support the thesis that people will learn from "doing what comes naturally," it can destroy training efforts by denying the need for them. The basic fallacy with this statement lies in the fact that it fails to consider the man who has had, instead of twenty years of experience, one year of experience repeated twenty times.

The aphorism "You can't teach an old dog new tricks" can be misused so as to destroy coaching efforts before they get started. It is often a defense mechanism used as an alibi for anticipated failure. And finally the old standby "Practice makes perfect" is still accepted as a basic truth. Of course, it is true that the person who practices is likely to become more skillful than the person who does not. But practice will not make a person perfect if he practices the wrong things. Or if he practices a procedure that is not the best one for getting the job done. Denny Roberts found this out in his efforts to become a better swimmer.

Practice will not make a person perfect
if he practices the wrong things.

When Denny was 18 years old, he considered himself a good swimmer, but he wanted to be a better one. He had an indoor pool available, so, every evening after school, Denny swam for an hour. Since he already knew the dog paddle and an overhand stroke and a convulsive leg kick, he practiced these. Denny practiced and practiced, but he did not become perfect. In fact, he felt a little annoyed by his lack of prowess when he compared it with that of Pat

Flanders, a classmate who also swam every evening. While Denny swam half the length of the pool, Pat swam the entire length and apparently did so with less effort.

Finally Pat said, "Denny, I notice you swim every evening but you don't get any better. How would you like me to show you some different things to practice?" "Like what?" asked Denny.

"The flutter kick, a smoother arm stroke, and how to coordinate your breathing with your swimming," Pat replied. "If you do, will I be able to swim as well as you?" Denny asked. "Not right away, but, if you keep practicing the things I show you, there's no reason why you shouldn't be able to eventually," answered Pat.

Denny did practice the things Pat showed him, and he did start to improve. Pat watched him carefully and offered suggestions on how to get more power from his arms and how to make a racing dive. Denny improved steadily. He didn't become perfect, nor did he become a champion, but he did learn that *what* you practice makes a difference.

All these half-truths are worse than lies. If they were out and out lies, at least we could denounce them without qualification. But because they contain an element of truth, they are accepted and, therefore, obstruct the efforts of coaches. In order to understand adult learning and to deal with it, it is essential to recognize all the obstacles to learning. These enemies of adult learning are effective primarily because many adults fear learning. Although many people find learning an enjoyable and satisfying experience, many others find the "joys" of learn-

Many adults fear learning.

ing akin to hitting themselves on the head with a hammer. Both feel so good when they stop.

There is something associated with the learning process that has made them wary of it. It is not essential for us, as coaches, to know why they feel as they do, just so long as we recognize this kind of attitude and know what to do about it.

And so our responsibility as learning practitioners (teachers, trainers, supervisors) is to answer the question, What can we do to help people learn?

26

In short, Chapter 1 dealt with some of the factors which affect the climate of the learning situation. If a supervisor is successful in taking the verticalness out of the work situation, then the fears and many of the inhibitions that obstruct learning will be eliminated. If a supervisor has adopted a Theory Y approach to management, he will be encouraging initiative and the attendant improvement of the employee. If a supervisor consistently adopts the role of a developer of his employees, he inspires constructive behavior. In this chapter, we have defined learning and have examined some of the obstacles that stand in the way of an adult learner. We are now prepared to consider the crucial question, How do adults learn?

3

How Adults Learn

BREAKING the material down into small steps is a teaching technique that makes learning easier. One of the reasons for the success of this is that when each step is presented as a small, realistically attainable goal, it does not seem so formidable.

THE NONTHREATENING APPROACH

Planning the learning experience in small steps is one of the basic approaches to adult learning. How many coaching efforts have failed because the change suggested has seemed too great? How many attempts at self-improvement have failed because people bite off more than they can chew? Adults learn in small steps. And if strong defenses against change have been built up, the first steps must be easily attainable, attractive, and nonthreatening. The poet Alexander Pope said almost 250 years ago:

> Men must be taught as if you taught them not,
> And things unknown propos'd as things forgot.

If the carrot is held too far out in front, it does not serve as a motivator. It is too far away to be easily attained, so it does not overcome inertia. In other words, a goal is not a goal if it is not realistic. And it is not a goal unless it is accepted as a goal. An improvement program is not a program of improvement if it attempts too much. To illustrate, consider the case of Jake Henderson.

Jake was a general foreman in a manufacturing plant and had worked in the same department for four years. In his annual performance review his superintendent, being an honest fellow, indicated that Jake lacked knowledge of the work but with instruction could be expected to improve in time. He also needed instruction and guidance in planning and organizing. His analytical ability was below average. He was slow in making decisions. He needed more drive. He was not as persuasive as he could be. He shied away from additional responsibility. He did not spend enough time developing subordinates. He was too blunt, often misunderstood. He could be more thorough in checking operations. He should take more interest in his work. In short, Jake's superintendent said that he needed more training in overall operations and more knowledge in handling men. Jake tried, but there was just too much that needed improvement. The steps were not small enough. Needless to say, little improvement resulted from this evaluation.

What might have been the result if one of these factors had been singled out and focused on? A person who understood that adults learn in small steps might have refrained from pointing out so many faults. A wiser supervisor might have focused his attention on one area for better results. He might have withheld all mention of the other areas needing improvement so that efforts, both his and Jake's, could be concentrated on the first step of an improvement program.

Even after a person decides to change and sets up a program for improvement, the first step is a big one. It is the one that gives adults the most trouble. So, the first step must be made easy and must not cause stress or it and subsequent steps will never be taken. But, if the first step is taken and if it proves to be a satisfying experience for the participant, he is more likely to take further steps. In fact, it may set off a chain reaction of progressively more difficult and more rewarding learning experiences.

For example, many industrial plants have found that educational classes will be well attended if they

are held on company premises in a familiar conference room, with colleagues for classmates and classes
scheduled soon after working hours. This combines
a maximum of convenience with a minimum of the
obstacles adults fear in education. This is an easy
first step to take, and, because it is first, it is vitally
important.

If university professors are called in to conduct
these classes, some of the participants might decide to
take noncredit classes at the university as a second
step. Even though the participants are then among
strangers instead of among their colleagues, many
will elect to take these evening classes. They will receive grades but, since they are not for credit, they
are not as threatening. After taking a number of these
classes, some people may decide to enroll in an
associate degree program. This is a "degree credit"
program, but it can be completed in half as many
hours as a bachelor's degree program. A recent study
at Southern Illinois University at Edwardsville
showed that this is the path of progress of many
adults. They can and do enter this continuum at any
point, but the vast majority enter at or near the
beginning—at the least threatening point.

So we see that adults move into and through any
learning experience with caution. This caution, char-
acterized by a reluctance to expose oneself to an
ego-threatening experience, causes them to take only
nonthreatening first steps, nonthreatening second

31

*Adults move into and through
any learning experience with caution.*

steps, nonthreatening third steps, and so on. Especially in the early stages of deliberate formalized learning attempts, adults learn in small, safe, easy steps.

LEARNING FROM THE ENVIRONMENT

Webster's Seventh New Collegiate Dictionary defines environment as "the aggregate of social and cultural conditions that influence the life of an individual or community." The coach must realize that he is a part of this environment, but only a part. To succeed as a coach, he must influence those portions of the environment which act upon the people he hopes to teach, because the learner tends to adjust his behavior until it is compatible with the changed environment. So the coach attempts to make adjustments in the "external conditions and influences affecting the life and development" of his subject. This establishes a new balance which includes the desired changed behavior.

Of course, the coach does not have total control of these external conditions, so his coaching efforts may take on the aspects of experimentation, with many errors of scale and direction. One of his main problems is that most situations involving the behavior and relationships of people do not lend themselves to tight control. Even his own behavior, which would seem to be under his own control, cannot be totally regulated. However, it is his own example, taken as a part of the total working environment, that is his most effective tool in bringing about behavioral change.

Important as his own example is, the coach's efforts must be consistent with the total environment. For example, it is difficult to teach neatness in messy surroundings, safety practices in a disorderly plant, or responsibility to a person whose peers regard responsible people as "squares." For example: A superintendent in an industrial plant found that his foremen were more successful in handling disciplinary problems after he replaced the clear glass in the four walls of the supervisor's cubicle with frosted glass. Before the glass was changed, a disciplinary problem evoked a display of sternness. The foremen put on a show of arm waving and finger pointing. After the frosted glass gave him more privacy, the foremen behaved more moderately. The superintendent had brought about a change in his foremen's behavior by making a change in the environment.

THE FOUR-STEP PROCESS

An important theory of adult learning known as the four-step process attempts to show precisely how learning takes place. It goes beneath the surface in an effort to explain what is actually happening when a person learns. We can best understand it by considering the case of Jimmy Jones.

Jimmy was a foreman in the processing department of a large chemical company. He felt a little uneasy about his costs. It seemed that every time he had a conversation with his boss, Emil Schroeder, it had something to do with costs; and it usually involved charts, graphs, and tables of figures. Sometimes Jimmy felt that he understood these figures while the boss was talking, but when he went back to his department they just didn't seem to apply. He noticed that the smart young college graduates could talk glibly about them and that they made a much better impression on the boss than he did. He figured that this was because the boss liked college graduates.

One day when Emil called him in to his office, Jimmy was not surprised to find that the subject was costs. Neither was he surprised when Emil held up a chart that showed that his costs were second highest in the division.

Even so, it bothered Jimmy and he found himself saying, "If you want to fuss about costs, why not raise Cain with Dan Houser? His costs are higher than mine and I don't hear you saying a word to him. In fact, all I hear is what a good job he's doing while I get chewed out because of my high costs."

"But, Jimmy, let me explain," said Emil. "Houser's costs are high because he is doing experimental work in his department that may save the company thousands of dollars if it is successful. In other words, we know why his costs are high, and, considering the experimental nature of the work, we think his costs are in good shape." "Well it still doesn't seem fair to me," said Jimmy. "Houser must have something I don't have, but I don't know what it is."

Emil held up the monthly variance report and said, "Maybe I can help you, Jimmy. When you look at these variance sheets, do you try to figure out what they show about the causes of your high costs? For example, do you realize that

35

this report shows that your loss and depreciation of direct materials cost almost ten times as much as the overtime your crew worked last month?" "Well, no. I didn't realize that," Jimmy replied.

Emil continued, "You've been doing a fine job of holding down your overtime costs. Now, if you could put an equal amount of effort into loss and depreciation, there is a possibility it could have ten times as much effect. If you like, I'll review these sheets with you each month. These college fellows understand all this, but there isn't any reason why you can't understand it as well as they do if you and I work together. And, with your greater experience in the department, you may be able to make cost reductions that they would never be able to match."

"I probably could beat them if I could just make sense out of those figures," Jimmy said. "How can you tell that L and D costs ten times as much as overtime?" "I'll show you," Emil answered.

After that they had several sessions in which they reviewed and analyzed the figures and then walked through the department looking at the high-cost items and discussing ways of reducing them. This was how Jimmy Jones learned how to control his department's costs.

Let's analyze just how Jimmy learned. First, he realized that he lacked something that he needed and that he should have. He knew it had to do with costs, but he didn't know exactly what it was. Note that this is more a feeling than a thought-out conclusion.

Second, Jimmy found out exactly what it was that

he lacked. When he said, "Houser must have something I don't have, but I don't know what it is," he gave Emil the opportunity to show him exactly what it was—the ability to detect from the figures the causes of high costs.

The third step in Jimmy's learning experience was that he decided he really wanted to learn this ability. And the fourth and final stage of learning came after Emil said, "I'll show you." The two of them took action.

Using Jimmy's experience as a model, we can generalize that the learning process actually consists of four separate and usually consecutive steps. The following breakdown was provided by Dr. Andrew Doyle of St. Louis University:

STEP 1. A person must sense in some way that he lacks something that he needs. This may be a bit of knowledge, a skill, a habit, or a developed ability to control oneself in order to perform more efficiently or at a higher level.

STEP 2. A person must understand precisely what it is that would fulfill his need.

STEP 3. A person must really want—intellectually and emotionally—and decide to obtain the knowledge, skill, habit, or ability.

STEP 4. A person must act to acquire this knowledge, skill, habit, or ability, and he must continue to act until he does acquire it.

SELF-ACTUALIZATION

These four steps deserve further study, but first there is another concept that influences their use. This is self-actualization, where everyone steadily and consistently tries to establish, support, and add to his image of himself. He may see himself as a man of action, an intellectual, an athlete, an artist, or a leader. He will willingly do those things that fit this image, and he will be unwilling to do those things that do not fit.

The concept of self-actualization requires a coach to present new learning so that it will help to establish, or actualize, the learner. This means that the learning should help the learner to use his potential —to put it into productive action. The learner should see that new learning would help him be what he has the potential to be—and what he wants to be. The coach, therefore, should present what is to be learned in such a way that the learner sees that it will benefit him to learn it. Emil chose just the right moment to tell Jimmy what it was Jimmy needed to learn (Step 2). And he told him in such a way that Jimmy could see that this would help him to become a more effective supervisor.

Self-actualization also requires that a coach or trainer present new learning so that it supports or maintains the learner. That is, a coach should make sure that new learning supports the learner's self-image rather than diminishes it. This is difficult for the coach to do unless he knows or feels what the

A coach should make sure that new learning
supports the learner's self-image.

learner's self-image is. For example, a few years ago management offered to train a limited number of union employees in work standards or job study engineering so that they could check the accuracy of disputed standards. However, when the word went out that this training often resulted in the employees' adopting the company's viewpoint, the training was not nearly so attractive. It was seen as detracting from, rather than maintaining or adding to, the employee's standing with his peers. In the case of Jimmy Jones, he felt that his self-image was threatened by the college graduates. In order to maintain and defend his self-image, he learned how to interpret the monthly variance report.

A coach must be alert to the possibility that a potential learner may see new learning as a threat, that it may force him out of the comfortable position where his self-image is fed and maintained. The concept of self-actualization requires that new learning be introduced so that the learner understands that it will enhance his self-image. It should make him feel greater in his own eyes and in the eyes of others— not only his colleagues but all people whose approval he desires. Establishing and supporting the individual's self-image is important, of course, but it would be even better if the learner felt that learning would *increase* the value of that image. Emil suggested that Jimmy's skill in interpreting variance figures coupled with his greater experience in the department would make him a more valuable employee than the men he considered his competition. Jimmy recognized this as an opportunity to better himself in his own eyes and in the eyes of others. Thus he had an incentive to learn.

Let us consider once more the four steps into which we have divided the learning process, but this time let us regard them in light of the concept of self-actualization. The trainer or coach must manage to get the learner to take the four separately identifiable steps. The coach must understand as best he can the self-image of the person who will take these steps. He must first bring about an awareness of the need for training. After all, it is difficult to convince a foreman that he needs instructions when he feels that he is already the best supervisor in the plant. It is necessary, first, to make him realize that he could learn skills or obtain knowledge that could make him an even better supervisor.

The second step for the coach is to make clear to the foreman exactly what the skill or knowledge is that he should learn. Vague suggestions, such as "Do a better job of controlling costs," are not enough. These may be adequate if the supervisor already knows how to control costs. But if the coach is to help the foreman by teaching him to control costs, he must show him specifically what must be done.

The third step requires that the learning be made acceptable to the foreman, both mentally and emotionally. If a foreman sees himself as the rugged he-man type, he is likely to reject requests that he become a better record keeper or typist. In this event, appeal to his desire for self-actualization through another channel. Perhaps he is striving to be a leader. If so, convince him that leaders control their groups by keeping adequate records. Learning must be emo-

41

tionally attractive—not threatening. And it must be safe and convey the possibility of prestige and gratifying accomplishment.

Finally, the coach must take the necessary action to help the person acquire the learning. In order to make it easy for the learner to acquire the skills he needs, the coach must make the learning situation as similar to the actual work situation as possible. If the coach tries to teach the learner to understand cost sheets, the coach must first show him how to read them, then let him read and explain them. This does not necessarily require close supervision in every case, but it does require enough supervision to insure that sufficient skill, knowledge, or habit is acquired to fulfill the responsibilities of the job.

4

Distinctive Characteristics of Adult Learning

ALTHOUGH most of the discussion up to now has been concerned with adult learning, many factors are sufficiently general to raise the question: Is adult learning different from child learning, and, if so, how? The answer is that adult learning is different in some ways.

TWO POWERFUL INFLUENCES

Adult learning is different from child learning in two essential aspects: First, adult learning is powerfully influenced by the past experience of the learner.

Adult learning is different.

Second, it is influenced by how the learner sees himself. We exclude those variances which may have a medical explanation and include only those people who are neither too young nor too old to learn. In short, we are dealing with the average child and the average adult.

An adult's learning is affected by his experience,

but since a child has had experiences also, the difference is one of degree. An adult identifies very strongly with his experience: "My experience is me. If you criticize my experience, you criticize me. I find it difficult to identify myself without referring to my experience. I am a newcomer, a veteran, a founder, a distillation department foreman, a sales manager, an X-ray technician, a hospital dietitian." These labels are partial identification of people; they are also statements of experience. Failure to recognize the importance of experience in adults jeopardizes any project in which adults are involved. But in a learning situation, it is particularly significant.

An adult's past experience may either help or hinder his learning. It depends on how his experience relates to what is being learned. If experience causes the adult to form conclusions or attitudes that conflict with the proposed learning material, obviously this will be a hindrance. If, on the other hand, his experience provides a vehicle for the accomplishment of one or more of the four steps of learning, this will be a help. However, much depends on the understanding, imagination, and skill of the coach. Great opportunities to apply this skill may be provided by the job situation if understanding and imagination can be brought to bear.

For example, it is generally assumed these days that engineers are poor writers. Although improvements have been made in college curricula in recent years, many engineers are still being graduated whose proficiency in writing is barely passable. Few engineers would include writing as the skill in which they are the most accomplished, and their supervisors would agree. Because of the great need for this skill, companies conduct in-plant training classes to try to improve it. One method of helping these men increase their competence in writing makes use of their past experience. They are shown that constructing a sentence is similar to constructing a mechanical device. They are urged to work on the construction of a paragraph or an entire report as a problem in engineering design. By doing this, they are able to call upon their experience in solving design problems and apply it to the specific problem of designing an effective sentence, paragraph, or report. Engineers understand this and respond favorably to it. They are pleased to find that they have writing skills they didn't know they had. In this instance, past experience helps learning.

Many times, however, past experience may hinder learning. This can be counteracted, though, if the coach is creative. Possibly the coach's most difficult problem is to change a person's habitual way of doing his job. Everybody develops a certain style, and changing it is extremely hard. Should we even try to change a style that is based on years of experience? The circumstances, the urgency of the situation, the nature of the people involved, and other considerations will influence this decision—and each case should be considered on its own merits. There is no general solution that can be applied across the board or even most of the time. But the question should be asked and answered in each individual case.

The main difficulty in changing an adult's habitual way of doing things is that over the years his experiences have reinforced his belief that he is doing things the right way. Whatever success he may have achieved he attributes to the validity of his methods and their applicability to all conditions. Every victory has reinforced this notion; every defeat is blamed on something else. If you wish to change a manager's style from Theory X to Theory Y, you must first overcome his conviction that Theory X is better. The longer the particular style has been used and the more often it has produced successful results, the more deep-seated is the belief that it is effective, and the more there is to unlearn before new learning can take place.

For example, suppose we want to teach a supervisor that absenteeism can be reduced by his sincere expression of personal concern. This supervisor has followed a lifelong practice of reprimanding absentees when they return to work, and he is convinced that in the past this practice has kept absenteeism under control. It should be apparent that before we can teach this man a new technique, we must first persuade him to stop using his old one. In effect, he must be taught to unlearn before he can learn.

The second major difference between the learning of adults and the learning of children is that adults see themselves differently from the way children see themselves. A child is dependent. He thinks of himself as a dependent person. He expects to be directed and to be told what to learn, and he accepts on faith that his role is subordinate to an adult's. An adult sees himself as an independent person. He expects to be self-directing and to accept responsibility. Further, he expects to choose what he will or will not learn.

Whereas the child learns for future use, the adult usually chooses to learn for immediate use only. The adult must see a clearly established need to learn. Where the child will learn to please his elders, the adult usually elects to learn only to please himself; that is, to satisfy a need which he has recognized and which he is convinced should be satisfied.

All his life the adult has been bombarded daily with thousands of sights, sounds, smells, feelings, facts, opinions, impressions, and conclusions to name a few. Because he is experienced, he has developed a system for filtering these bits of information. He cannot allow himself awareness of all of them, so his protective filtering system automatically selects certain types of information to get through to his consciousness. The owner of this device can tune in and tune out at will. Moreover, the experienced adult is more likely to use the device when he sees an immediate use for the information.

An example of the importance of this factor in adult learning is the case of a training program for a group of department managers, which was presented in two one-day sessions one week apart. At the end of the first day the participants were asked to evaluate the day's activities. Their comments indicated that the program was "interesting" but that they didn't see how they could use it. Informed that next week's one-day session would make it clear how all the information tied in, they were not convinced. Their filters had already been put into use. And even though the next session did show the connection between their jobs and the material presented for learning, the damage had already been done. Barriers had been constructed. Decisions not to learn had been made—subconsciously, but surely. The result was that neither session was as effective as similar sessions conducted by the same leader on the same subject where an early connection was made between conference material and the job.

We can conclude from this example that adults enter a learning activity with the intention to apply what is learned. Because of this, successful adult learning is usually problem-oriented. Growing awareness of the advantages of problem-oriented adult learning has found expression in the case-study method, in-basket training, the incident process, and other such forms. Advocates of these methods are so devoted to them that some declare that judgmental matters can be taught in virtually no other way. "Learning by doing" is the credo, and, where doing requires the exercise of judgment, the problem solving is essential. Short of experience on the job itself, almost the only way to sharpen judgment is to exercise it by solving problems. The coach on the job has the advantage of having real-life cases to use for teaching.

So we see that adult learning must be problem-oriented, but there is a further requirement: The problems must be realistic. Many adults, even after making a commitment to learn, refuse to study something they consider unrealistic. For instance, in a course in industrial psychology designed and presented specifically for industrial foremen, a standard college introductory psychology textbook had been used. The foremen rejected the textbook. A complaint voiced by many of them was, "We don't want to learn about rats. We want to learn about people!" The textbook was dropped, and after an extensive search a replacement was found which used industrial, in-plant work-situation examples. It was geared to the same level and taught the same things as the original college textbook, but the foremen considered the examples more realistic. They therefore accepted the learning material, and there were no complaints.

A more extreme example took place in an in-plant training program for riggers in a steel mill. The class was in blueprint reading, and the specific problem was to teach an appreciation of perspective. The instructor used the familiar example of railroad tracks, showing how the rails appeared to get closer together as they faded into the distance and how the telephone poles alongside were represented by progressively shorter lines as the distance from the viewer increased. The following day the union steward who represented the riggers lodged a complaint. "We don't work on railroad tracks. We're riggers, and we want to learn to read blueprints about rigging."

SKILLS ARE LEARNED BY DOING

Even though the adage "Practice makes perfect" leaves a great deal unsaid, it is worth noting that skills are indeed learned by doing. Although practicing the right procedures makes a tremendous difference, the fact remains that the one indispensable ingredient in the learning of a skill is performance. If you want to learn a skill, you start by doing it, and you keep doing it, hopefully under the guidance

51

Skills are learned by doing.

of a qualified coach, until repetitive practice and coaching improves your performance to an acceptable level of speed and accuracy. When this state of proficiency is attained and the performance of the task becomes habitual, it is said that you have learned the skill. Of course, not all learners level off at the same degree of proficiency, but no one ever expected that they would.

The skills that are learned by doing are usually thought of as manual skills. But nonmanual skills such as supervisory skills, selling skills, teaching skills, can also be learned by doing. From the standpoint of learning, *skills are those activities which can be made to conform to habit-controlled patterns.* This is a broad definition, but it does encompass the vast majority of adult activities either on or off the job.

We are concerned with on-the-job activities, most of which conform to habit-controlled patterns. A lawyer is said to be unusually able to sway a jury. We hear of people who have learned to read a thousand words per minute. A foreman may have developed the extraordinary ability to get his work group to be enthusiastic about a project. Even though these activities require no manual dexterity, they generally follow habit-controlled patterns, so we consider them nonmanual skills.

We call someone skilled at performing a task—either manual or nonmanual—when the performance becomes habitual. An understanding of this is essential to an understanding of how adults learn. Take the example of learning to drive a car. When first viewed, driving a car seems to consist of a series of separate manual tasks each of which produces a result. Each task must be carefully considered along with its possible consequences, and then it must be carefully performed. The learner must first check to make sure the gear is in "neutral" or "park"; then he must insert the key into the ignition (making sure to select the proper key); he must then turn the key clockwise, listen for the motor to start, and then release the pressure on the ignition key. The learner continues: He must listen again to make sure the car is running; look ahead, behind, and to the sides to make sure it is safe for the car to move forward. He reaches for the gear shift, moves it to "drive," and

53

so on, and so on, with tedious and painstaking attention to detail. How different this is from the actions of an experienced driver. What happens to these details after we learn to drive? It is as if some other person inside us takes over these tedious tasks. We seem to be relieved of them completely and permanently. We are now skilled. We do them by habit; that is, we no longer need to think about them. In fact, many of us have had the experience, during a long drive, of having passed through a town with no recollection of having passed through it at all, even though we had stopped at the right places, observed speed limits, and met all the other requirements of safe, responsible driving.

Skills really are learned by doing, and awkwardness gives way to effortless proficiency as repeated performance permits habit to take over the details of a task. But what is often not fully realized is that this marvelous service is not free. We pay a price for it. As we permit the subconscious, or whatever we may choose to call it, to be accountable for these chores, we find that we have forfeited our "right to manage." We have committed ourselves to using the accustomed method for the rest of our lives—or until we can persuade this servant-turned-master to permit a change.

In understanding how adults learn, it is essential to realize that each of us is not entirely his own master. Each person lives to some degree under the control of a tyrant and thus is limited in his freedom to change. Although he may want to change, he may not be able to. He needs help to overcome an old habit and to replace it with a new one. Moral support and encouragement are important, but they are not enough. Replacing old habits with new ones requires understanding. Those who have dedicated themselves to helping the victims of the more destructive habits such as alcoholism and drug addiction have learned a great deal about understanding. They have learned that an understanding of the habit itself is vital. They have also learned that a sincere desire on the part of the one to help and on the part of the other to be helped is essential to success.

At first, new habits may be formed by repetition even before the old habits are rooted out. Therefore, it is often helpful if new procedures are tried on a tentative basis. Thus the way is left open for the person to back out. Otherwise his sense of security may be jeopardized and his incentive lost. He needs time to get used to the new procedures and to form new habit patterns. Many successful innovators will introduce a change with the request that it be tried for a short but definite period. This allows time for the new habit patterns to form and for the initial awkwardness to wear off. Nearly always, the new method or behavior will not feel as good as the old method, simply because the old one is familiar and the new one is not. Take the case of Billy Bishop.

Billy was a ten-year-old boy who liked to play baseball. One day his father, watching him at bat, said, "Billy, you're holding the bat cross-handed. A right-handed batter should grip the bat with his right hand over his left hand. You're doing just the opposite. Hold the bat the other way and you'll not only hit the ball more often, but you'll hit it harder too."

Billy tried the new grip, but it felt awkward. He noticed, however, that everybody else batted that way. He even studied pictures of major league players, and, sure enough, they held their bats the way his father said. This presented quite a problem to Billy. He wanted to change, but when he tried the new grip he felt tense. It took all the fun out of playing, and the only reason he played ball was for the fun of it. But striking out wasn't much fun either, so he decided that in spite of the feeling of awkwardness and self-consciousness he would change.

A few days later, he found himself getting base hits and at the same time enjoying the game. Then, just to test, he tried batting cross-handed again. It felt awkward. He knew he would never go back to cross-handed batting.

Habits make valuable servants. But they also make formidable adversaries. It is good for a coach to know that learning often requires that an old habit be defeated so that a new habit may be mastered.

In sum, many supervisors expect that their employees will modify their behavior to conform to a directive as soon as the directive is received, and that henceforth this modified behavior will continue without deviation. However, if we accept the idea that adult learning includes action and is a modification of behavior through experience, then we must also accept the fact that it takes time. To show that a change in behavior has, in fact, become habitual would of course require several observations made over a long period of time. The processes of thought and understanding, of action and reaction, that are necessary to achieve a change are referred to as *learning* a new procedure.

But there are many obstacles to this learning, many fears to be overcome, many intellectual and emotional criteria that must be satisfied in order to accomplish it. Adult learning is powerfully influenced by past experience. It is just as strongly influenced by the fact that an adult sees himself as an independent, self-directing person. Immediate and meaningful application of the new procedure is important, if not indispensable. The coach must understand all these influences on adult learning if he is to help adults develop their full potential.

The Framework
of Coaching

WHAT is on-the-job coaching? What can coaching
do? What is the role of the coach? What devices can
the coach use? The answers to these questions are
essential to an understanding of the coaching process.
They might be thought of as the framework of coaching. They constitute the strong elements of the coaching structure. They are not the whole of coaching,
but they are fundamental parts of it. Let us consider
each of these questions in turn.

WHAT IS ON-THE-JOB COACHING?

Now that we have considered the nature of the supervisor-subordinate relationship and have reviewed some of the processes through which adults learn, a supervisor, teacher, trainer, or coach is ready to assimilate these matters into the coaching itself. For our purposes, *on-the-job coaching is personnel development, planned and performed in the workplace.* It includes evaluating people's skills and abilities in order to identify their strengths and weaknesses. It also includes determining together—both coach and learner—just what the learner needs in order to meet the requirements of the job. A plan must then be formed to fill those needs. Finally, it includes follow-up to make sure the plan accomplishes its purposes. As implied in Chapter 1, the province of on-the-job coaching lies in the area between the actual and the ideal; that is, it concerns itself with closing the gap between the person who actually holds a specific position and the person who would be ideal for that position. This requires an evaluation of what the man on the job is doing and the establishment of some standard of what he is expected to do.

On-the-job coaching requires an answer to the question, When is the job well done? Is the job well done when all specific duties have been satisfactorily

On-the-job coaching requires an answer to the question,
When is the job well done?

performed? Is it enough that only the work assigned
by the supervisor be performed? Is more required
than this? Is creativity necessary? Do we require that
some initiative be exercised before we say that the
job is well done? Suppose a display of initiative
makes us uncomfortable. Does this mean that the
job is not being performed well because the incum-
bent shows too much initiative? We need *realistic*
criteria in order to coach effectively. Finally, on-the-
job coaching deals not only with improvement on
the present job but also with preparation for future
jobs. In this regard, identifying and preparing for

a specific future job will better focus the coaching effort and thereby make it more effective.

WHAT CAN COACHING DO?

Having defined on-the-job coaching as personnel development in the job situation, we now come to the question, What can coaching do? It can help us with the job of "getting things done through people," which is the classic definition of management and which is not a completely adequate definition for those of us who work in organizations. (The definition does not apply to a person managing an investment account with virtually no contact with people, or to a farmer practicing crop management and doing all the work himself.) Whether we are or aspire to be members of management or whether we manage the business of a union, a sales district, a hospital floor, or a governmental agency—no matter what kind of organization we serve or where we fit into it—we can understand our organization better if we see that the function of its management is to get things done through people. For an example of how coaching can help us get things done through people, consider the case of Ray Hillman, manager of the services division of a large hospital.

Ray urged Phil Buchanan, his laundry supervisor, to take a night course in management practices where the principles

61

and techniques of planning, organizing, and controlling were emphasized. Ray suggested that he meet with Phil once a week to discuss the new ideas and techniques that Phil had studied in the course. At one of these meetings, Phil reported that he had studied cost reduction. "That's great!" said Ray. "I've been thinking that cost reduction is one of our primary failings. Did you get any ideas as to how we can reduce costs in your department?" Between them they worked out a cost reduction program they thought Phil could apply. Phil did apply it, and it did reduce costs. Ray came to consider Phil his cost reduction expert, and he referred other cost reduction problems to him and helped him solve them. As a result, Phil became the best cost reduction man in Hillman's services division.

What can coaching do? Effectively performed, it can help people develop to their full potential. If supervisor and subordinate agree in advance that a new skill is needed, and the subordinate goes to the trouble of learning it, it is likely that this skill will be used. The kind of coaching that Ray Hillman did, with organizational and individual goals reconciled, can help an organization get things done through people and can be a boon to the supervisor as well, because he is rewarded for getting his job done better. He uses coaching as a tool for effective management.

In addition to helping a supervisor get his job done better, coaching often brings other rewards. These may be subjective benefits such as inner satisfaction, the respect of peers, and the gratitude of those people helped. This was true in the following case:

A group of successful salesmen who had been called together for a company conference were relaxing between sessions when somebody mentioned Sherman Graham, a salesman who had recently retired. "I certainly hope he is adjusting well to retirement," said one salesman. "I feel that whatever success I have, I owe much of it to him. When I was just a young kid, I spent almost three years working with him out in the boondocks, and that's when I really learned this business."

"You, too?" said another. "I had almost the same experience and with the same result. If it hadn't been for Sherm, I doubt that I would still be in this business." As others spoke up, it developed that every man in the group had worked for Sherm and that each credited him with being largely responsible for the contribution that each man had been able to make to the progress of the company and toward his own progress. Apparently Sherman had achieved a reputation as a developer of salesmen early in his career, and someone in the company had been astute enough to make full use of his skill.

Sherman may have felt rewarded by the knowledge that he had helped many salesmen reach self-actualization. He may also have felt rewarded by the respect he had of those he had helped, by an awareness of his splendid reputation, and by the confidence that he had earned it. He could not spend these rewards because they were all intangible—they were feelings that existed inside him. As for tangible rewards, we do not know to what heights in the organization Sherman might have risen if he had regarded the younger men he helped as competitors and had kept his wisdom and knowledge for his own exclusive use.

WHAT IS THE ROLE OF THE COACH?

The framework of coaching may be subtly influenced by changes in the nature of the supervisor's organizational role. These changes appear to take place slowly but their effects are beginning to show in some organizations. These changes seem to have been brought on by the rapid increase of technological developments, by the growing acceptance of McGregor's Theory Y, and by the growth and liberalization of motivational theory.

Once supervisors were heard to boast that "There's not a single job in my department that I can't do myself." But nowadays it is essential that they supervise jobs requiring skills and technical knowledge that they do not possibly have the time to acquire. Organizational requirements sometimes make it necessary for a man to supervise several such highly technical and highly skilled positions at the same time. He could not know all the jobs or all the skills. He may find it almost impossible to tell which job is the most difficult, or which requires the most skill, or the most knowledge. Yet he must somehow judge how well each job is being performed.

Are there any differences between the way a supervisor goes about performing his job under these circumstances and the way he would perform if he were able to do every job? Indeed there are, and these differences affect his coaching efforts as much as they affect the other phases of his job. He must share the planning and controlling functions with the technicians he supervises. The specialized knowledge the technicians possess is essential to both planning and controlling. So these functions are performed jointly.

In addition to the differences brought about by advanced technology, there are also differences that reflect the ascendancy of Theory Y and differences that attest to the motivational value of worthwhile goals. Add to these the increasing demand for self-actualization, and we have a trend toward a new role for the supervisor which places greater emphasis on helping his subordinates. As this trend gathers momentum, the supervisor's role as coach is altered to accommodate the changes. The supervisor is less the fatherly coach passing on hard-gained advice on how to do a better job and is more a partner in planning and goal setting. The result is reduced verticalness and increased horizontalness; less application of Theory X and more application of Theory Y; less decision making by a single person and more interdependence; decreased separatism and increased communication; less paternalism and more joint planning.

Setting Objectives

An important part of the coach's role is his responsibility for setting objectives. "A job well begun is halfway done" may be an exaggeration, but it points up that the planning and initial steps of any project are of major importance. The objectives should be clearly defined, perfectly understood, and accepted by both supervisor and subordinate. This is more likely to occur if both have a hand in establishing those objectives. The supervisor may be reluctant to permit the subordinate this latitude lest the wrong objective be chosen. Actually, the supervisor has little to lose, for if he selects the "right" objective but the subordinate does not accept it, little progress will be made. Once the objective is set, a plan is made for carrying it out, and its implementation is scrutinized daily, the job of helping an individual to develop may indeed be "halfway done."

Identifying Coaching Opportunities

Another part of the coach's role is his responsibility for identifying coaching opportunities. Just as a well-drilled football team is able to take advantage of the breaks, and sometimes even create the breaks by aggressive play, so a development team made up of a supervisor and subordinate who know what they want to accomplish can sometimes create coaching opportunities and can often take advantage of unforeseen occurrences when they arise. An objective and a plan of action would, in fact, increase the likelihood of this development team's taking advantage of unforeseen occurrences. It would enable the team members to recognize early an opportunity when it presents itself and to fit a change into the plan.

Identifying these coaching opportunities is, of course, a skill in itself—a particularly useful skill to an on-the-job coach. There are few guidelines, if any, to help him. Success depends primarily on constant awareness, which seems to be best cultivated by a clear understanding of what one is looking for. The most commonly used device for identifying coaching opportunities is the performance appraisal. It serves as a reminder to both supervisor and subordinate of the desirability of making improvements, points out weaknesses and strengths, and, more often than not, tends to lead to the creation of an improvement plan.

In recent years, performance appraisals have been used and abused, "cussed" and discussed, and have been as much maligned and misunderstood as they have been praised and appreciated. Despite this ambivalence, and despite supervisors' perfunctory attitude toward them, performance appraisals seem to be here to stay. This is generally attributed to two factors: (1) the well-documented and established belief that people want to know where they stand with their boss and (2) the fact that appraisal interviews insure at least one annual coaching opportunity. There is much to indicate, however, that the coaching opportunity is often skipped or lost in the conflict that results from an attempt to justify a rating. This is especially true where ratings are related to salary increases. Even so, a coaching opportunity is provided. And maybe even more important, appraisal interviews afford an opportunity for setting objectives and making plans. If the supervisor and subordinate take advantage of this opportunity, then the actual coaching can be done on a daily basis in the job situation.

When coaching, supervisors seem reluctant to enter into frank and open discussions. There is no mystery about this, however. Many coaches have a natural hesitancy to discuss any delicate subject, especially an emotional one, whether their comments be complimentary or uncomplimentary. Getting coaches to coach has been and is now a difficult problem, and we need not look beyond our own feelings for the reason. Viewed in this light, it is apparent that many coaching opportunities are lost because the coaches do not want to see that they are there. However, coaches who do recognize the opportunities and who have a developmental objective and plan for each employee hold the key to successful coaching.

WHAT DEVICES CAN THE COACH USE?

Any practice that is part of a plan to help an individual improve is a coaching device. Anything a supervisor does to help a subordinate develop is a coaching device. Anything a subordinate does which is encouraged by the supervisor to help the subordinate develop is a coaching device. The intent of the action determines whether or not it is a coaching device. For example, giving a subordinate a task that he has never performed before without giving him instructions is a coaching device if it is part of a plan intended to increase his self-reliance. If there is no such plan, then such an act might be considered bad management. Whether or not it was a good idea would depend upon its outcome.

The most important point to be made about the following procedures or techniques is that they may or may not be examples of coaching. It depends on whether they are a part of a plan for the individual's development. If they are performed accidentally, they are certainly not coaching. If they are performed incidentally—that is, for some purpose other than for the individual's development—they are not coaching.

69

Coaching is neither accidental nor incidental. It is deliberate and should have a purpose. (In our list and discussion of the various devices that can be used in on-the-job coaching, there are some that are not discussed.)

Special Projects

If a worker is assigned a special project because he has less work to do than other people or because it is convenient for the person who assigned the project, then this is just a special project—an assignment of extra work—and nothing more. However, in an area where improved skill or additional experience is deemed necessary or desirable for the subordinate's development, the assignment of a special project could be used as a coaching technique. If the assignment is made (preferably by mutual agreement) for the purpose of providing this experience or for learning a skill, gaining knowledge, or changing a habit pattern, it may be a good coaching technique.

For example, a foreman is concerned because he knows little about budget preparation. He has told his supervisor that he wants to learn more about the subject. The supervisor agrees that this is important, and so he assigns the foreman the task of assisting in the preparation of the next departmental budget request. The foreman is to try to learn some budget

*The assignment of a special project
could be used as a coaching technique.*

techniques from reading and from experienced
budget men. He is then to prepare a preliminary
draft of a budget request and discuss it with his supervisor, explaining how he arrived at each figure.
Together, they revise the preliminary estimate and
prepare the final draft.

In some instances, these make-work projects are
justified. However, with a little imagination a supervisor who is aware of the problems of the organization as well as the developmental needs of his
employees should be able to create a situation that

71

would benefit both the individual and the organization.

Job Rotation

Consider the case of Charley Jenkins.

Charley supervised a production department consisting of 26 men, one of whom was his brother-in-law Steve. Steve had had special training that qualified him for a highly skilled job, and, in the normal course of events, he had gotten himself transferred to Charley's department. The plant manager felt that having two men so closely related in the same department was a bad idea, especially since one of them was the other's supervisor. The difficulty was that, because of the scarcity of men with the particular skills involved and because of contractual seniority agreements and other complications, it was easier to transfer Charley than it was to transfer Steve. So Charley traded sections with another foreman in the department.

Contrast this with the case of Pete Porter, salesman.

Pete and Barney, his sales manager, had annual appraisal interviews in which they assessed Pete's progress in relation to his objectives, set some new objectives which they worked out together, and discussed Pete's weak and strong points. Pete said that he hoped to be a sales manager himself someday. Barney said that he thought Pete should have some experience in the division sales office. This would help him understand and appreciate the supporting activities that go on in the office and would teach him how to use those activities to give maximum help to the field salesmen. Pete agreed that, even though he liked his present territory, he would welcome the opportunity to broaden his experience. Four months later a vacancy opened in the division office, and Barney urged Pete to take the position.

These are two cases of job rotation accomplished for two different purposes: one for the convenience of the company, the other for the development of the individual. We would expect that the different purposes would result in a different outcome. Surely Charley Jenkins' supervisor would not be surprised if Charley fails to show as much stimulation and improvement as Pete Porter, even though the action in both cases was the same: Each man changed his job. In Charley's case it was a matter of convenience; in Pete's case it was part of a development plan where there was a purpose.

Professional Societies

Sometimes membership in professional societies is tolerated by an organization simply because it keeps the company's name in the minds of the other society members. This is particularly attractive when those members are prominent businessmen. Other organizations encourage their professional employees to be active in certain societies for reasons of prestige, to "show the flag." And still others discourage membership because they believe that close association with people in other companies will lead to the exchange of information on salaries and job openings with a consequent increase in dissatisfaction and turnover.

Many conscientious coaches believe that membership in professional societies helps the development of their young professional employees.

George Kessler's boss, William Hogan, suggested that George, a young training director, join the American Society for Training and Development, because William thought that membership would have a stimulating effect on George's growth. It did. It also exposed George to dozens of new training ideas, some of which he was able to apply on his job. When he had a training problem, he was able to discuss it with older training directors who had solved similar problems. He served on committees and was elected to various offices. In this way George gained experience as treasurer, secretary, program chairman, director of a one-day conference, and president of the local chapter. These experiences added tremendously to his self-confidence and to his ability to chair meetings, coordinate planning for an organization or a project, and accept responsibility for a cooperative effort and follow it through to completion. All this added significantly to the contribution that George made to the progress of his company.

Thus, encouraging young men to be members of a professional society is an effective coaching device when the coach's intention is to develop his employees' abilities and, in the long run, to make valuable contributions to the company.

Formal Classes

Though not normally thought of as a coaching technique, formal classes are often used as part of a supervisor's total coaching effort to help a subordinate develop. As with the preceding examples, the effectiveness of this effort may depend, at least in part, on its purpose. For example, a few people attending university night school classes may be doing so in order to achieve the prestige that goes with a college degree. On the other hand, take the example of John Schmidt.

A year ago, John, a brilliant young engineer, was promoted to the position of head of the industrial engineering department in his company. Since that time he found that he did less and less of the engineering work for which he had been trained and more and more management work, for which he had not been trained. As a result of a discussion with his plant manager, he enrolled in a management development program in order to learn the fundamentals of management which he needed on his present job. John knew what he wanted out of the program and expected to apply immediately some of the management principles he learned.

There is such a wide variety of adult education classes these days that a supervisor and employee who have identified an area of need can usually find a night course to help them with their improvement program. Supplemented by daily contact on the job, these courses can be quite effective as a coaching device.

Vacation Replacement

The day may come in the life of a supervisor when he finds that his own career advancement depends upon the capabilities of his subordinates. An effective coach might handle the problem by having one of his subordinates be his vacation replacement as part of a development program. The supervisor might consider, for example, that if one of his subordinates had to take over his job, he would need to understand the workings of the shipping department. His replacement must understand the nature of the pressures that sometimes converge upon the shipping department—what it can mean when 25 trucks show up for loading on a day when 15 were required; what it can mean when two or three large customers call on the same day to ask for quick shipment of an order; what can happen if somebody does not make sure that warehouse stock is rotated. The supervisor, taking all this into consideration, might make the vacation replacement assignment that will best fit the development program of one of his subordinates.

Representation of the Supervisor at Meetings

A manager often finds that he simply cannot attend all the meetings he is expected to attend. But he may need to know what goes on in these meetings, and it may be important that his department be represented to insure that its interests are protected. The responsibility for attending meetings can be and often is assigned to a subordinate who needs the experience. He may need to learn to feel at ease with the higher-echelon people who attend these meetings, to increase his ability to communicate with them. He may need to learn more about the processes within the formal organizational structure. It may be of developmental benefit for him to find out how decisions are made, how information gets to the decision makers, what kind of information they pay most attention to, and who has influence and who does not. It may, in short, give the learner information which can help him to become better acquainted with his own company.

Committee Assignments

As a coaching technique, delegating committee assignments closely resembles substituting for the boss in meetings and can yield similar benefits. In fact, the benefits here may be even more far-reaching because there is a continuity about a committee assignment which permits practice in planning, preparation of recommendations, and, in many instances, follow-up. Unfortunately, in many cases, expediency becomes the governing factor, and whoever can be spared is usually the one who is assigned. But committee assignments can be used as coaching tools if they can be made to fit into the improvement plans of employees—if they are developmental in purpose. With forethought, and assuming the existence of predetermined individual objectives, they can be made to contribute to a person's progress.

6

Three Coaching Strategies

WE have seen that an in-depth understanding of the coaching process depends upon the answers to the four key questions: What is on-the-job coaching? What can coaching do? What is the role of the coach? What devices can the coach use? These questions and their answers have given us a framework for coaching. Now let us use this structure as a base for our study of coaching strategies.

For our purposes we can define a coaching strategy as a *large-scale plan for improving the performance of an individual.* The coaching devices referred

79

to in Chapter 5 can be thought of as tools or small-scale plans which can help to implement a strategy. That is, a small-scale plan may be used to carry out a large-scale plan. A coaching device can be used to put a coaching strategy into effect.

The coach cannot use all the devices at once. Even if he could, he would probably succeed only in confusing himself and the person he is trying to help. How then can he use these devices so that they will be most effective? Although the practitioner will have to decide this question for himself in each case on the basis of his evaluation of each situation, the following are strategies which may help clarify his role and responsibilities as coach. A supervisor can

1. Try to change the environment and thereby change a person's behavior.
2. Consider coaching as a matter of reward and punishment.
3. Prescribe and supervise certain key points.
4. Encourage joint planning.
5. Control the rate at which a subordinate takes on responsibility (and the amount of responsibility he takes on).
6. Concentrate on a subordinate's strengths and weaknesses—coach the extremes—developing the former and eliminating the latter.

Three of the strategies are described in detail in this chapter. The other three are discussed in Chapter 7. Although in practice the strategies overlap, they are discussed separately here in order to help the practitioner identify them clearly.

CHANGE THE ENVIRONMENT

Even though changing the environment was discussed in Chapter 3, it is reintroduced here because it is one of the six basic approaches to coaching. Some people say that changing the environment is the most important factor in changing a person's habitual behavior. This is based on the idea that it is natural for a person to adapt and respond to his environment. No matter how his behavior seems to others, to him it seems reasonable, rational, and responsible. Since he sees no flaw in his behavior, he does not expect to change unless and until something in his environment changes. When that happens, he will observe the change, evaluate it in terms of what it means to him, and, if he feels so inclined, react to it.

A coach who elects to change his subordinate's environment assumes that the changes he makes will bring about a different kind of behavior. If they do not, or if the changed behavior is not what the coach wanted, then he can try other changes in the environment and observe their effects. This continues until the desired behavior is adopted.

For example, if a girl spends much of her time

81

talking, her supervisor might try moving her next to a noisy machine where talking would be more difficult. If this does not work, he might try telling her that her peers and her supervisor do not approve of her because of her excessive talking. At this point the coach may well find himself thinking, "All right, I realize that a change in environment would be a good way to change her behavior, but how can I do it?" Are there ways a supervisor can go about making changes in a person's environment and, if so, what are these ways? Some answers to this are

- Rearrange or replace furniture.
- Relocate or replace equipment.
- Reroute the flow of work.
- Change the general surroundings—paint, lights, temperature, furnishings.
- Make personnel changes.
- Make organizational changes.
- Move to new quarters.

An example of a coach changing an employee's environment is illustrated with the case of Pete Kozak and Charley Davis.

Pete Kozak, maintenance superintendent, wanted Charley Davis, a tool design technician, to make himself more available to people with tooling problems. Charley's desk was in the tool crib. He liked being near his tools, and it was apparent that he preferred to associate with the tools rather than with the people who had tooling problems. Pete believed that this limited Charley's usefulness and inhibited his chances for personal growth. Talking with Charley had failed to bring about any change in his habits.

Finally Pete decided to change Charley's environment. Pete moved Charley's desk into the shop office, where he still had access to his tools, but they were not at his elbow. When people came into Pete's office with a tooling problem, Charley became involved. Almost at once he was making a greater contribution to the organization, and gradually he became more people-oriented as he acquired more experience in helping them. By changing Charley's environment, Pete had both improved the service of the maintenance department and added to Charley's personal growth.

Here is another example.

Myron McDaniel was a troublemaker. His job allowed him contact with practically every other person in his department. He loved to talk with his fellow employees, and, in order to hold their attention, he would tell them all the unfavorable things he heard in the course of his rounds. If somebody thought he had received a raw deal from the company, McDaniel not only circulated the story, he improved on it.

From his foreman's viewpoint, there were three things wrong with this. (1) It seriously interfered with McDaniel's work. (2) It kept the rest of the department in a state of turmoil. (3) It fostered an attitude that would prevent McDaniel from being promoted to a more responsible job. The foreman knew what the trouble was, but he was unable to find a solution. Penalizing McDaniel for not getting his work done only gave him more disruptive news to circulate and just made the situation worse. Finally, in desperation, the foreman rearranged the workplace so that a single operator worked in an isolated spot apart from the others. He gave this operator's job to McDaniel. Set apart, where he could not talk to the other employees, all McDaniel could do was work. Not only did he work, but he learned to like it. Furthermore, when he met the other employees at lunch or in the washroom, he did not have a tale of woe to relate. He was no longer a troublemaker. And a serious impediment to his possible growth had been removed by a change in his environment.

Another example of changed environment making a change in a person's habitual behavior is the case of Susie Ellison.

Susie started working when she was 18 years old in a small office where Edith, the senior secretary, was a woman of 50. Old enough to be Susie's mother, Edith assumed a protective attitude toward Susie. After five years she still treated Susie like a little girl, and because of her example everybody else did the same. Susie never really learned the office procedures because Edith always took the initiative. This was the easy, comfortable way for both. The result was that Susie never learned to take responsibility or exercise initiative.

The office manager, Vic Siegel, recognized that Susie had potential but that her relationship with the older woman was preventing her from developing it. He decided to put Susie in a position where she did not have Edith to lean on. So when it became necessary to move a man in Vic's office upstairs where he could be near the vice-president, he convinced Edith to go along as his secretary.

This left Susie in charge of the office. The prospect of having to assume responsibility frightened her, but the other members of the office for whom Susie did secretarial work started treating her as a responsible person. She responded to this change in their attitude and to the change in her position in the organization. She learned the office procedures and began to contribute to the improvement of operating practices. She began to exercise initiative and to take responsibility. Thus Vic was able to improve Susie's performance and personal development by changing the environment.

These three examples illustrate how coaches can influence employees' behavior by making changes in environment. Such changes can be made by rearranging or relocating furniture or equipment as in the case of Pete Kozak, by rearranging the flow of work as Myron McDaniel's foreman did, or by making a change in personnel or organization as in the case of Vic Siegel.

USE REWARD AND PUNISHMENT

The oldest and most elementary way of changing habitual behavior is to reward desired behavior and to punish undesired behavior. This strategy is one of the most effective ways of getting quick results. It assumes, of course, that the coach has the power to dispense rewards and punishments. It also assumes that the behavior the coach wants to produce is indeed the right behavior; the trainee has no choice in the selection of behavioral goals. This basic and

*The oldest and most elementary way of changing
habitual behavior is to reward desired behavior
and to punish undesired behavior.*

straightforward approach is probably in widest use
today.

Some supervisors wish that they had absolute
control over rewards and punishments for their workers, especially when they have tried unsuccessfully
to push through a raise, a promotion, an extra day
off, or some special privilege for an employee; or
when they have been frustrated in their attempts to
force an employee to change. Every supervisor can

reward and punish to some extent, and if he does both in a consistent and timely manner, people will be inclined to do what will be rewarded and not to do what will be punished.

For example, the master-apprentice arrangement mentioned in Chapter 1 was a relationship based on the principle of punishment and reward. When the apprentice failed to perform his job in accordance with the high standards set by the master, he was punished verbally—without fail and without delay. When he performed well, he was rewarded by being praised or by being respected by the master. The apprentice was, therefore, conditioned not only to meet high standards of performance but also to abide by rigid standards of conduct.

One common mistake in coaching is the failure of the coach to take into full consideration the powerful influence of rewards and punishments. A coach must be realistic about the goals he sets for himself and for the people he coaches. If he is trying to develop behavior that the work situation does not reward, he may have a hard time. He will have an even harder time if the work situation not only fails to reward but actually punishes the type of behavior he is trying to develop. The case of Ben Tyler illustrates this point.

Ben was general foreman in a production department, and he had a problem with costs. According to his boss, costs were too high, and something had better be done about it.

As Ben studied the cost figures, it became apparent that the main reason for excess cost was the unusually large labor pool that was maintained to cover absences in the work-force. The plant had far more absences than the national average, and his department rate was 50 percent higher than the plant average. Obviously, this was the place to start solving the problem. Foreman Joe Radcliff's section had the highest rate of absence. After discussing the problem with Joe, Ben decided that Joe wasn't tough enough. There were instances in which men had been absent and Joe had done nothing about it. Obviously, Joe needed some coaching on how to deal with absenteeism. "Rewards and punishments," thought Ben. "That's the key to dealing with this problem." He said to Joe, "From now on, Joe, I want you to follow company policy to the letter. The second time a man is absent, he gets a one-day layoff. The third time, he gets a three-day layoff."

"But, Ben, we haven't been following that policy," protested Joe. "Nobody in the whole plant actually follows that procedure." "That's just the trouble," growled Ben. "It's time we started following procedure. It's company policy and has been for four years. So let's follow it. I don't believe in having rules you don't follow. We've got to start tightening up on enforcement." "If I do start following it, will the company back me up?" Joe asked. "Of course the company will back you up," Ben snapped. "It's the company's policy and the company is paying you to enforce it. The fact is, the policy was made to protect you, the foreman. So it goes without saying that the company will back you up."

The next day one of Joe's men was absent. It was actually this man's sixth absence in recent weeks. After each previous absence, he had been warned, but not laid off. When he returned to work this time with no excuse, Joe called him into the office. Joe explained that he was forced by necessity to be more firm about enforcing the absenteeism rule. He filled out the prescribed form for a three-day layoff, explaining that this was in accordance with company policy. Later that day he was presented with a formal grievance requesting that the penalty be rescinded. Joe denied the grievance, but when it was appealed, his decision was reversed and the employee was paid for the three days he did not work.

Joe went to Ben's office and said, "Ben, I know you've been wanting me to get tougher on absenteeism and, basically, I think you're right. But when I follow your advice, I get punished. I think we need to talk about this. I'm confused."

Ben had tried to change Joe's way of dealing with this problem. However, the work situation not only failed to reward Joe, but actually punished him for following the course of action Ben had recommended. Foremen often feel that management has given up most of its options for rewarding good work and for punishing poor work. It is true that management's prerogatives have been restricted, but the prerogatives still exist. A foreman does retain power to reward and punish. Because of the restrictions, it is necessary that he use more skill, imagination, and consistency in applying these rewards and punishments. He needs to have a firm understanding of what he can do and cannot do. In the interest of thoroughness and of his own effectiveness, he needs to be aware of the alternatives.

The coach must determine, first, what alternatives are feasible and, second, which of these he prefers. In making these judgments it may be helpful to consider the following lists of possible rewards and punishments. Any or all of these may be available to a supervisor to some degree at one time or another.

Rewards	Punishments
Praise of work.	Condemnation of work.
Withheld punishment.	Withheld praise.
Increased respect of peers, supervisors, and subordinates.	Decreased respect of peers, supervisors, and subordinates.
More opportunity for earning self-respect.	Less opportunity for earning self-respect.
Decreased tension.	Increased tension.
Improved communication.	Decreased communication.
More recognition.	Withheld recognition.
Higher salary.	Decreased opportunity for earnings.
More privileges.	Fewer privileges.
Greater freedom of action.	Less freedom of action.
Expressions of esteem.	No expressions of esteem.
Increased responsibility.	Decreased responsibility.
Promotion.	No promotion.
Expressions of confidence.	No expressions of confidence.
Increased opportunities for achievement.	Decreased opportunities for achievement.

Selecting from among these possible rewards and punishments (and others not listed here) requires an intimate knowledge of the situation at hand, a good understanding of the people involved, and an indispensable factor—sound judgment. A coach picking at random from this list would be no more likely to pick a winning combination than a carpenter who picks tools at random from his toolbox while blindfolded. Selecting the right coaching tool for the job to be done is an essential ingredient of good coaching as the following example illustrates.

Joe Black, production superintendent, was trying to help Harry Vogel learn how to make out the weekly production schedule. Joe had tried telling Harry, condemning his errors, and even hinting at possible promotions if Harry could learn to do it well. This combination of rewards and punishments had not produced the results Joe was looking for. After two months Harry still wasn't able to make a workable schedule. So Joe decided to select rewards and punishments that related to peer group approval and disapproval. When Harry developed a schedule that was awkward to work with, Joe asked one of Harry's co-workers, "How did you like that schedule? I understand it put your section in a bind." Harry, seeing that this was true, realized that an awkward schedule caused hardships among his co-workers which resulted in their decreased respect for him. When the schedule improved, Joe was careful to make sure that his peers gave Harry the credit for it. This soon got the desired result. Harry checked his schedules out with his co-workers to make sure they were satisfactory and workable before he turned them over to Joe. When Joe realized that

Harry was doing this consistently, he knew that he didn't have to worry anymore about that job being done properly. He realized that he had finally selected the right combination of rewards and punishments for effective coaching.

SUPERVISE KEY POINTS

The third coaching strategy is that of encouraging the practice of specific key points. Key points are not the main steps in the operation but those points of skill and judgment, of safety and efficiency, which are so critical in the performance of the job that they deserve special emphasis. These points would not be readily understood or perceived by the novice unless they were specifically pointed out and emphasized by an experienced person. And these are the points which perhaps one time in a thousand may spell the difference between success and failure—between mediocrity and excellence.

It is because these key points make such a difference in overall performance that this approach merits more serious consideration and wider application in job situations than it has received in the past. An encouraging factor, a surprise to many who have not tried the key-point approach, is that most jobs involve only a few of these key points—often only five or six of real significance. And they can be taught to a subordinate.

*These points would not be readily understood
or perceived by the novice unless they were
specifically pointed out and emphasized
by an experienced person.*

Jim Hanes attributes much of Bob Peterson's effectiveness in making cost presentations to the coaching he did
when Bob was new on the job. As the new supervisor of the
cost analysis section, one of Bob's duties was to make a
weekly cost analysis presentation to a group of executives.
If this was not one of his most important duties, it was
certainly the one that was most noticed. Jim realized that
Bob would be judged largely on how well he performed this
particular part of his job. Bob's first presentation did not go
well, although he was thoroughly prepared. Jim felt that
Bob realized this, and would be receptive to some coaching.

"Bob," he said, "you have the same problem I used to have.
You are naturally a quiet, unassuming guy who does his
job thoroughly and well, and it is not a part of your nature

93

to wave your arms and get bombastic and emotional when making a cost presentation. However, when I first started conducting sessions similar to the ones you are responsible for now, I realized that if I just stood up there and spoke in a quiet, unassuming way, I wouldn't get my message across. I never went into one of those sessions when I didn't have an important message to communicate, and half the time I didn't get it across because of my manner. I was serious, but nobody knew it but me.

"So," Bob continued, "I developed a new way of acting in front of groups, and this is what I suggest you do. I practiced certain key points: I would raise my voice to emphasize points that I thought were important. I would vary the tone of my voice. I would use gestures. I would move around a little. Give them some action. These were the key points. You know how people act when they are overenthusiastic? When they get excited? Well, I would practice doing this. Of course I didn't do these things all the time; that would be monotonous. I varied it. I watched the eyes of people and adjusted my actions according to what I saw in their eyes. At first I would pick out four or five to watch, but as I became more skillful I found that I could maintain eye contact with many more. Maintaining eye contact is a key point also. You might try some of these things, Bob, and see what kind of results you get."

Bob was not wholly convinced. "I'm afraid I'll feel like a phony," he said. "Like you, it's not my nature to wave my arms and make a big show." "I know it isn't," agreed Jim. "But it is your job to get your message across. Those charts and graphs you draw are fine. But they're not enough. You must develop a more interesting manner. By that I mean a manner that can get attention and keep it. That takes skill and you don't learn a skill by doing just what comes naturally. You must keep experimenting until you have developed a manner that you can use when you need it. Don't worry; it won't change you. It will just help you express what you think needs to be expressed. Try some of these key points next week and let's see how they work out."

Bob did try them and reported to Jim that he had felt awkward, just as he had anticipated. And he had felt phony. However, he did feel that he had communicated better than he had the week before. In fact, he felt a certain inner satisfaction from seeing his audience react. He realized he was making his audience understand hard-to-express points. Jim offered a few suggestions and praised him for having the courage to experiment. The following week Bob did even better. After a few weeks he reported that practicing the key points seemed less and less like a put-on and was becoming a tool that he could use when he needed to make people understand. Jim noticed that Bob seemed to be more self-confident, that his cost presentations were better understood, and that they got the desired action.

Many supervisors do not use the key-point strategy of coaching as much as they might. They tend to associate this strategy with athletic and manual-skills coaching. They fail to see that mental skills are as susceptible to this strategy as the manipulative skills since mental skills can be taught step by step, through key-point coaching, just as manual skills can. The experience of Karl Kraft may also help to illustrate how identifying and practicing key points may be an effective coaching strategy for developing mental skills.

Karl was supervisor of several foremen in an industrial plant in which the hourly workers were represented by a strong and militant union. One new foreman in particular, Ron Reynolds, seemed to suffer from a lack of self-confidence. Karl thought this was caused partly by inexperience with the technical requirements of the job, partly by a lack of confidence in his own decision-making skill, and partly by fear of the union. Ron had been a member of the union until he was promoted, and he knew he would have to return to it if he did not succeed as foreman. Karl knew that he had to build up Ron's self-confidence if Ron was ever to be an effective foreman.

Karl called Ron into his office to talk about the situation. After he and Ron agreed that Ron had a lack of self-confidence and after they had verified that the key points Karl had identified were the reasons for it, Karl said, "Ron, I want to tell you how the Navy helped me develop the mental skills I needed to gain self-confidence in standing deck watches. Maybe we can use some of the same ideas. In an emergency on a ship at sea, if the officer of the deck does not take prompt and correct action, the consequences can be quite serious. I think that you are uncomfortably aware of the fact that lots of things can go wrong in your section. Like the officer of the deck, you must act quickly and correctly if anything goes wrong with the process, the equipment, or the men. This awareness is causing you to be very tense and unsure of yourself. Am I right?" "That's exactly right," said Ron. "I'm afraid I'll do the wrong thing or that I won't know what to do, so I do nothing, and that's even worse than doing the wrong things."

"O.K.," said Karl. "This is the way the Navy helped me develop the mental skills I needed to overcome the same feeling. My senior officers taught me a mental exercise which amounts to a continuous drill on emergencies. Whenever I was not actively engaged in doing something else, they would create imaginary emergencies for me to solve. Things like 'Man overboard, starboard side. What do you do?' Or, 'You lose all electrical power. What do you do?' Then they encouraged me to put problems to myself. After a while I had imagined and worked out solutions for about every problem I could think of. You'd be surprised what it does for your self-confidence when you have developed your mental skills to the point where you have an answer for every problem that you can imagine.

"Why don't we try that with your job, Ron? Let's set up hypothetical problems about your job—the technical requirements, the decision making, and dealing with the union. Let's make it a sort of game, O.K.? Who is your best operator? He quits. What do you do? A process operator stays on the job but disobeys your orders. What do you do? Every man in your section demands a transfer. What do you do? Quality suddenly drops below standard. What do you do? A man gets his arm caught in a machine. What do you do? From your viewpoint what would be the worst thing that could happen in your section? It happens. What do you do?"

Over the next few weeks Karl and Ron played this game, each trying to think of a hard technical problem, a difficult decision to make, a tough union problem. They did not always agree on the best solution, but they worked out something. As Karl expected, Ron's self-confidence rose as his problem-solving skills developed. After a while his self-confidence was no longer a matter of concern to either of them.

97

In these two examples the coach identified and then worked on key points. When these key points were dealt with properly, performance levels rose. These points dealt with mental skills, and the coach was able to transfer his own skills to his subordinate through supervised practice. This process is key-point coaching.

7

Three More Coaching Strategies

SINCE the coaching process is highly personal, there is no universal formula that applies to all coaches in all situations. Three more of the coaching strategies mentioned in Chapter 6 are detailed here so that coaches can have even more alternatives to choose from.

ENCOURAGE JOINT PLANNING

Another strategy for coaches is joint planning. The value of the joint-planning approach to coaching is that, if plans are made by coach and subordinate together, and the only plans adopted are the ones acceptable to both, each person will benefit. The coach will have an opportunity to influence the selection of objectives, to help put the plans into effect, and to enjoy his subordinate's improved performance. The subordinate will have a chance to exercise self-direction in the choice of objectives, to receive his supervisor's help and attention in putting the chosen plans into effect, and to improve his own performance.

The basic concept of this strategy revolves around the idea that all development is self-development and that a person will change his habitual behavior only when he is convinced that a change will be beneficial to him. This is not to say that some unconscious and unnoticed changes will not occur. But it does mean that conscious changes will succeed only when they are planned by the subordinate himself.

In Chapter 3, four steps are listed in the learning process. A person (1) must feel a need, (2) must identify exactly what will fill that need, (3) must want whatever it is that will fill the need, and (4) must take steps to get it. All these involve action or thought on the part of the learner. In other words, nothing that the coach does will make his subordinate a better worker, a better planner, or a better supervisor unless the coach's influence causes the subordinate to take some action himself. Only the subordinate can improve himself, because his learning depends on his active involvement. The learner is, of course, committed to his own ideas and will follow his own plans with more confidence than he will follow the plans of others.

Like other approaches to coaching, this strategy is not new. However, it seems to be gaining in favor in the United States as the management process evolves from authoritarian to democratic. It relates especially well to Theory Y, which is based on the idea that a person will exercise self-control and self-direction in working toward objectives to which he is committed. Some companies ask each employee in a responsible position to prepare a list of his objectives for the coming six months. His supervisor reviews the list and may then offer suggestions before the objectives are adopted. Employees are encouraged to include personal development objectives as well as organizational objectives. Once adopted, they become official, and their progress is measured at the end of the six-month period.

Some supervisors and subordinates prepare their own personal schedules showing the progress they expect to make in certain time periods. Progress is checked at the beginning and end of a scheduled period, and regular checks are made along the way. This gives the supervisor more opportunity to help his subordinates. It is also helpful if some means of objective measurement can be devised and agreed upon, because if progress can be quantified, it can be more easily measured against a time schedule. In any event, objective measurement is desirable. It reduces the possibility of a person's being judged partially and subjectively, which is a constant threat to the climate of helpfulness and approval. It emphasizes results, forces planning of specific goals, and is generally regarded as fair.

Identifying and using objective measurement raises the questions: Is there evidence that improvement is needed? What is the evidence? How can this evidence be measured? Is there enough evidence to show that this specific improvement is needed? If improvement is made, will it be reflected in the evidence? The supervisor may be forced to ask himself: Does the job require this particular improvement, or is it simply my own personality that requires it? Sometimes a supervisor wants an employee to change his behavior simply because the supervisor cannot adjust to a particular personality trait in the employee. When objective measurements are established, this useless personal indulgence is eliminated; emphasis is on the evidence, not on personalities.

This emphasis carries over into the progress interview. A beneficial side effect of focusing on the evidence is that it tends to direct the interview into a discussion of the *job* rather than the *person* doing the job. This permeates the entire interview, minimizing the possibility of defensiveness, arguments, and the consequent lack of constructive accomplishment.

Joint planning depends on both people really wanting to participate in the planning. It depends on a feeling of equality and mutual responsibility. If joint planning does not seem appropriate to one or the other of the two people, it may be that this feeling has not been established because of one of the following reasons: A supervisor may have such a strong sense of his own responsibility to plan that he finds it difficult to accept the ideas of others. Or a subordinate may be so used to vertical relationships that he finds sharing responsibility unacceptable. With someone like this, the coach would do well to try a different strategy. Most people, however, accept joint planning and react favorably to it. Take the case of Paul Wilson.

Paul worked for Adam Schwartz for about six months when one day Adam said, "Paul, you have been doing a good job of getting all the things done that need to be done each day, but I'm concerned about the future. You've been doing your job well, but I'm not sure I'm doing all I should to help you develop. I have a responsibility to you that I want

103

to be sure I'm meeting. You may have some ideas about this yourself. Let's get together after lunch and work out a plan for the next six months."

After lunch they met in Adam's office and made some plans. Adam emphasized two purposes: The first one was to get the job done, and the second was to develop Paul. They discussed plans that would improve both the job and Paul. Adam saw to it that the plans were realistic. As he put it, "We don't have to shoot for the moon, but let's put some stretch into our plans." They did just that and finally decided exactly what their objectives would be.

A job-related objective was to bring the department up to date on engineering changes. There was a backlog of 50 engineering changes to be made, and this backlog indicated that Paul needed some development in scheduling and follow-up. They decided, first, that once they were notified of engineering changes by the central engineering department, they would make the changes within one week of receipt of notice, even if they had to work overtime to do it. Second, they divided the changes into major and minor categories according to the amount of work each change appeared to require. Then they decided to install five minor changes per week for a period of eight weeks and one major change per week after that. Following this schedule, Paul would complete all changes eight weeks before the six-month target date. Both were satisfied that this was enough of a cushion to allow for unforeseen difficulties. Adam felt that, if this plan resulted in their meeting their target date, Paul would come to appreciate the value of good scheduling and follow-up.

An objective relating more directly to Paul's personal development was for him to learn to write better reports and letters. They agreed, first, that Paul would do more writing to give him more practice and, second, that he would submit all rough drafts of reports and letters to Adam. Adam would coach him on organizing and wording, make suggestions for changes, and explain his reasons.

When Paul left the meeting, he felt good about the contributions he had made to the overall plan, and he felt a certain excitement about the possibilities the plan held for his own development. He and Adam prepared a follow-up schedule for reviewing progress at two-week intervals during the six-month period, and Paul felt reasonably sure that if anything interfered with their progress along the way, they could work out some way of meeting the target dates together.

Adam had created a situation where equality in planning, mutual reponsibility, and involvement were possible. And Paul had responded to this situation with better on-the-job performance and personal growth.

CONTROL THE RATE A SUBORDINATE TAKES ON RESPONSIBILITY

Coaches who control the rate at which a subordinate takes on responsibility, and the amount of responsibility he takes on, believe that people generally rise to any occasion. These coaches feel that when more is demanded of a person, he shifts to another gear and performs at levels higher than ever before.

They believe in pressing for near-peak performance but without forcing a subordinate beyond his capabilities.

Coaches press for near-peak performance but without forcing a subordinate beyond his capabilities.

Managers of professional prizefighters are some of the most successful practitioners of this brand of developmental brinkmanship. When Muhammad Ali (Cassius Clay) fought Ernie Terrell, Ali had a record of 27 wins and no losses. Terrell's record was 39 wins and 4 losses. How did these men arrive at the top of their chosen professions with such impressive records? Certainly not by easy victories. Managers know that if a boxer beats only easy opponents, he does not develop, nor does he rise to the top. The point is to have your man fight bouts that result in hard-won victories. Each match must provide a challenge. The possibility of failure must be present. The challenge must make the fighter extend himself to the limit in order to win.

Successful managers are careful not to press too far or too fast. They avoid having their fighters suffer defeats because of the psychological effect they might have on the fighter. After all, it doesn't take many defeats to convince a man that he is no good. And, at least in theory, the man who has never known defeat is more confident than the man who has. He expects to win, and this is important in a champion.

There are many managers in business, industry, and government who apply this approach, with some variations, to personnel development. They assign a man responsibilities and watch how he handles them. Then, before he grows comfortable with them, the managers assign more difficult responsibilities. Using the same concepts as the fight manager but a different vocabulary, the supervisors attempt to insure that each assignment will provide progressively more "stretch" in the job. (The term "stretch" has recently become a part of business jargon. When managers say "We have to build some stretch into the job," they mean the same thing as fight managers when they say "We match him so he'll have to fight hard to win.") All approaches vary, but the results are generally the same: For example, one industrial manager said, "In our company we use the modified sink-or-swim method. We make a new man sweat, but we don't let him fail." Another said, "We put a man into a position where he will make some small mistakes. If he doesn't make a few mistakes, he doesn't learn." Another industrial coach referred to a "delegate but help" procedure, "I give a man plenty of responsibility to challenge him," he said, "but then I help him when he needs it so that he is able to get the job done satisfactorily and on time."

One common complaint among college graduates joining companies in recent years is that they have been assigned make-work projects—that is, projects that keep them busy and out of the way until they have been around long enough to learn the ropes. The company's idea is that their being present for a period of time will make them aware of whatever is necessary to help them meet responsibility when it is assigned.

The graduates, however, feel that their work is not really necessary and, therefore, that their employers do not have confidence in them. This reduces their self-confidence and causes disillusionment and discontent. If they are assigned this make-work over a long period of time, the graduates may learn to expect failure, and this attitude may help bring about failure. In recent years many companies have taken into consideration this commonly voiced complaint and have revised their policies regarding work assignments for newly hired college graduates. They have found that people develop faster and better when responsibility is generously assigned. But the responsibility must be real; the job must be genuine. Just as in the case of the developing prizefighter, the possibility of failure must be present. Not necessarily failure itself, but the possibility of it.

Using failure as a teaching device is advocated by some people, but it is greatly overrated. "Let him fall on his face a couple of times. He'll soon learn." This is a variation of the sink-or-swim philosophy, and it has little to recommend it. A man who has failed may know something that the man who has not failed does not know, but it is knowledge that the undefeated man may be better off without. A manager of a prizefighter would not deliberately overmatch his protégé on the theory that he would learn something from being beaten. True, he would learn how unpleasant it is to fail. But this is precisely what the coach does not want him to learn, because this learning would inhibit action and increase caution. So the person being developed would be wiser but less effective. Failure does indeed teach quickly and well, but what does it teach? Is the lesson it teaches worth learning?

People learn from small mistakes. They also learn from total failure. The successful coach must decide which knowledge is more valuable. He must also have an objective in the development of the person he coaches, and he measures all that person's learning against his obective. It is in this way that he lets his pupil make some small mistakes but not large and costly failures. The coach may let his pupil come close enough to failure to recognize it but still not let him fail. As with the manager of a prize-fighter, the skill is to provide the protégé with experiences that make him stretch but not fail. Deciding how much and how fast responsibility is to be assigned requires judgment, skill, and awareness.

CONCENTRATE ON STRENGTHS AND WEAKNESSES

Coaching efforts can be effectively applied by concentrating on a subordinate's strongest and, in some cases, weakest points. The strongest points should receive attention first. The weakest points should receive coaching attention only if they are below the supervisor's tolerance level. Otherwise they would receive little or no attention.

It seems that the most effective coaching is performed when the coach has an objective. What should this objective be? In what area should we concentrate our coaching efforts in order to bring about the most beneficial changes in a subordinate's habitual behavior? The traditional answer to these questions is: Locate the subordinate's weakest point and try to improve that area. For example, if a

*The weakest points should receive coaching attention
only if they are below the supervisor's tolerance level.*

hospital supervisor's weakest point is getting along
with his employees, then he should be coached in
human relations. If an industrial foreman's weakest point is his understanding of the process he is
supervising, then he should be coached in the mechanics of that process. If an office manager's weakest
point is getting reports out on time, he should be
coached to develop ways to insure that he gets his
reports done on time.

111

This approach is not only traditional, but it seems logical. As a matter of fact, it sounds so reasonable that to suggest a departure from it would seem to be folly. Yet coaching efforts so aimed do not always meet with success. We are prompted to ask, then, Is there a better way?

Most of us are aware of our own strengths and weaknesses. What are you good at? What are you not good at? What kind of work do you do? Why do you do that kind of work and not some other? If you are a research scientist, why are you not a salesman? Do you feel that you are better qualified to do research than to sell? If you are a salesman, why are you not a post-office supervisor? Is it circumstance only, or do you feel that direct selling makes the best use of your particular combination of strengths and weaknesses? If you are a foreman in a metalworking plant, why are you not a laboratory technician? Is it only because on the day you applied for work there was an opening in production and none in the lab, or does your personality better fit production work? All of us have certain abilities and inabilities, certain strengths and weaknesses. Why do we have our own particular set of likes and dislikes rather than someone else's? Why did we develop certain preferences? Can it be that, without realizing it, we have been directing our lives to make the fullest use of our strengths while avoiding pursuits that would point up our weaknesses?

Each of us has spent a lifetime developing strong points and learning to accommodate weak points. This is how we have coached ourselves and managed our own development—we've built on our strengths. Yet we try to develop others by concentrating on their weaknesses. And, not surprisingly, we have been more successful in developing ourselves than we usually are in developing others, because we have used one method for ourselves and a completely opposite method for others: One concentrates on strengths; the other on weaknesses.

So we have a partial answer to the question, "Is there a better way?" It would be better to develop strengths rather than weaknesses. It seems the natural system to follow since we have all been following it for ourselves. Certainly it is an effective system. Whatever success we have is partly, or even mainly, a result of this system. Following this reasoning, we could say that, for a given amount of coaching effort, we would have better results by concentrating on a pupil's strengths rather than on his weaknesses.

When we start using this technique, we find that it actually changes the coaching relationship. Several things will be different: First, the subordinate will be more at ease and receptive, because his strong points are emphasized instead of his embarrassing weaknesses. Second, the coach will have to use more skill, because it is more difficult to suggest ways to improve an already strong point than it is to find

113

fault in areas of weakness. Finally, we will get more cooperation and will be more effective because we will be helping our subordinate do the things that all of us tend to do—build on our strengths.

This coaching technique, however, does not necessarily solve the problem of the hospital supervisor whose weakest point is human relations, or of the foreman who does not understand a process, or of the office manager who has trouble getting his reports out on time. Their weakest points are still weak, even though they may be making progress in the development of their strongest points.

One weakness may prevent a person from gaining rewards he deserves for his many good characteristics. For example, the weakness of the hospital supervisor, the foreman, or the office manager may keep each from realizing his full potential. He may have all the other characteristics needed for success, but if the one weakness is far below the generally accepted tolerance level for his job, he may not be able to perform the job adequately. Or he may not be permitted to advance. The consequences depend on how pronounced the weakness is, how important it is, and how great the difference is between his actual level of performance and the minimum acceptable level for the job.

There is sometimes confusion about the minimum tolerance level—not only about the level itself but especially about how it is established. It should

114

be set by the job itself. However, it is more than likely that the personal feelings of the immediate supervisor will have a great deal to do with it. The supervisor might do himself a favor by questioning whether it is his personal prejudice that makes him decide that a person's performance is inadequate or whether it is the requirements of the job itself. If it is his prejudice, he may have set unreasonable standards for the job. In that case, what may be needed is not a change in the employee's behavior but a revision of the standard.

For example, in the case of the hospital supervisor who does not get along well with his employees, what exactly is acceptable in his working relationships? What are the symptoms of inadequate performance? What is the evidence? What is the minimum amount of improvement that would be acceptable? Does this inadequacy seriously impair the supervisor's effectiveness? How much? Is he getting an adequate job done in spite of it? Is the present situation tolerable? If so, the coach should concentrate on the supervisor's strong points. If not, the coach should help the supervisor develop his abilities in human relations.

With the foreman who has inadequate knowledge of the process he supervises, how much knowledge would meet the minimum requirement? Is this lack of knowledge a real handicap, or is it only that the foreman's supervisor, having a thorough knowledge

115

himself as a result of long service, cannot bear the thought of a less well-informed person occupying the position? Is the present situation tolerable? If so, the coach should concentrate on the further development of the foreman's strengths. If not, then a coaching procedure should be set up and pursued until job knowledge reaches the minimum acceptable level.

In the case of the office manager who has trouble getting reports out on time, how serious a fault is this? How late are the reports? How important is it that they be on time? How often are they late? Does the job require absolute and inflexible promptness, or is there a tolerance factor of a day or two? Does the job require that the reports never be late, or is this an obsession of the office manager's supervisor? Is the lateness caused by some flaw in the habitual behavior or attitude of the office manager? Is the present situation tolerable? If so, the supervisor might direct his coaching efforts more effectively at the strong points of the office manager. If not, he should try to improve this weakness.

In summary, the concept of coaching the extremes suggests that attention be given first to the strong points of the person being coached, with attention being given to his weaknesses only if they cause performance to fall below the tolerance level, not of the supervisor, but of the job. Attempts to improve strong points will yield greater results per unit of effort than attempts to improve weaknesses, because everyone is accustomed to developing his strengths and has a built-in resistance to recognizing and working on his weaknesses. Even so, if performance in some areas is below the level permissible for the job, the coach must take action to increase effectiveness in these areas. When the tolerance level is reached, development efforts should shift to the individual's strong points.

The six coaching strategies outlined in Chapters 6 and 7 are not mutually exclusive. It is not suggested that one approach be used and the others excluded. They represent different ways of thinking about the problem. They are described separately to give the on-the-job coach assurance that there is more than one way to approach any coaching situation. If one strategy does not suit his style or does not work, he should choose another. This increases his versatility as a coach and will increase his chances for success.

8

Specific Coaching Situations

NOW that the nature of the supervisor-subordinate relationship has been explored and adult learning behavior, the framework of coaching, and six basic strategies for coaching have been discussed; what else can be offered to the person who is striving to become a better coach? What additional exercise does he need to make him a master at developing men and women? A coach may find it necessary to deal with many different situations and the following cases are examples of some of these situations. They are included to stimulate the coach's mind and give him the confidence of one who has thought about a subject in depth.

COACHING'S COMMON DENOMINATORS

In a sense, every coaching situation is special and personal. It involves at least two people, each of whom is unique. Even so, there are certain common denominators which can be identified, certain attitudes which are found in more than one instance. It may be helpful to (1) discuss some of the most common of these, (2) emphasize the importance of being a good listener, (3) consider interviewing as it relates to coaching, and (4) offer some cases as exercises to increase a coach's second-hand experience.

The Coach as Listener

As a prelude to the cases, let us first consider the attitudes and abilities of the coach himself. Surely they are no less important to effective coaching than the attitudes and abilities of the person being coached. The supervisor's sensitivity to the needs and feelings of others, his empathy, and his listening ability are important ingredients in a coaching relationship.

119

The first thing to recognize is that taking an interest in the details of other people's lives is hard work—and listening conscientiously is hard work. Yet, in order to have a good climate for coaching, it is

*Taking an interest in the details
of other people's lives is hard work.*

important that the coach listen to the other person's point of view. Often a decisive factor in the listening climate is the coach's sensitivity to his subordinate's minor daily needs. Fortunately, this sensitivity feeds the coach's interest in his subordinate, his interest makes listening easier, and listening heightens sensitivity. The entire cycle increases trust and openness for both coach and subordinate.

The other side of the coin is that the more open a person is, the more likely he is to say what he really thinks. This happens because he trusts the other person more and, therefore, is willing to expose more of himself. But, in exposing more of himself, he risks more; namely, disagreements, hurt feelings, estrangement, and tension. Tension is not all bad, but it is a factor with which both supervisor and subordinate must learn to cope. If they do, the tension can become a constructive force. It can lead to a fuller discussion of differences. And, as these differences are better understood by both persons, more satisfactory and productive working relationships can be established. An important part of this sensitivity depends on listening. Since there is a good deal of literature offering advice on how to listen effectively, it is not detailed here. However, the coach would do well to consider that listening is a skill that can be cultivated and improved like all other skills. Although it would be an oversimplification to say that one can listen more effectively by merely deciding to do so, the listening a coach needs to do depends primarily on a desire to understand what another person is trying to communicate. Desire is the main ingredient, but practice is indispensable. The supervisor who wants to improve his coaching skill will do well to practice his listening skill.

The Interview in Coaching

Like listening, interviewing is a topic about which a great deal has been written, and so it is mentioned here only for the purpose of emphasizing certain phases of it as they affect coaching. Not all coaching devices involve interviewing. However, most coaching does depend upon a face-to-face, one-to-one confrontation which may be broadly referred to as an interview.

Performance appraisal sessions. Although it is not the only type of interview in existence, the most commonly thought of and most commonly used type is the performance appraisal interview. This is the session held periodically in which supervisor and subordinate sit down face to face and the supervisor—while trying to establish and maintain an atmosphere of openness, frankness, and free two-way communication—reviews the performance of the subordinate. It often happens that the chemistry of this situation causes the interviewee to become defensive. The interviewer says something that is interpreted as a criticism, and the subordinate feels called upon to defend his action. Once defensive action is begun, it is very likely to continue. Unless extreme skill is exercised, supervisor and subordinate become adversaries. Each adopts emotional objectives and finds it difficult to admit that anything he says is wrong or that anything the other person says is right. In any case, there is no turning back, and this is sometimes referred to as an irreversible process.

Once the irreversible process has been started, only specially trained people can stop it. For the average person, the only solution is to avoid getting into it. While there is no guaranteed formula for this, it is true that results are better in situations where the interviewer is the interviewee's helper, not his judge. If the interviewee is convinced that the interviewer is actually trying to help him, he does not become so defensive. This allows attention to be focused on plans for improvement and usually results in a more constructive coaching interview.

One procedure which has been used successfully to reduce the probability of defensiveness is for supervisor and employee to prepare separate forms and then meet to discuss their differences and similarities. This can be done with the appraisal interview form used by most companies or with the forms shown in Figures 1 and 2. The form used by the employee is shown in Figure 1 and the form used by

Figure 1. Special appraisal form for employees.

Personnel Comparison Checklist

Both employee and supervisor fill out a form. Then the two meet to compare lists and to work out a program for improvement based on those areas where agreement is reached.

Name_____

Job_____

Employee's Questionnaire

1. In what areas would you like to improve?

2. In what areas of operation would you like to take a more active part? Less active part?

3. In what areas should your relationship with your supervisor be strengthened?

Figure 2. Special appraisal form for supervisors.

Personnel Comparison Checklist

Both employee and supervisor fill out a form. Then the two meet to compare lists and to work out a program for improvement based on those areas where agreement is reached.

Name_____

Job_____

Supervisor's Questionnaire

1. In what areas would you like to see this employee improve?

2. In what areas of operation would you like to see him take a more active part? Less active part?

3. In what areas should your relationship with this employee be strengthened?

the supervisor is shown in Figure 2. Such check-lists can help a supervisor avoid evoking an attitude of defensiveness in his employee. Another way to prevent defensive behavior is to avoid mentioning salaries, so that the main thrust of the interview can be directed at improvement, not money. If the supervisor allows an appraisal interview to become a salary review (and, unfortunately, most companies do not separate the two) the chances for any construc-tive plans are greatly reduced. The interview may deal with other subjects first, but, once the subject of money is introduced, no other subject receives seri-ous consideration—no matter how long the inter-view lasts. This is not to imply that salary should never be discussed. It means that salary and improve-ment are almost mutually exclusive and that you can discuss one or the other but rarely both in the same interview.

Some companies have solved this dilemma by having a joint planning session at which only achievements and plans are discussed. Salary discus-sions are separate and are held periodically and as far removed as possible from the joint planning ses-sion. A simple but effective form which can be used in the annual appraisal (not salary) interview is shown in Figure 3, which was designed and used by Gerald T. Canatsey of Pet, Incorporated.

No matter what forms are used as guides for these planning and discussion sessions, it is important that

Figure 3. Annual appraisal form.

Personal Data Sheet
_____
for
Annual Evaluation of Personnel
_____
(Confidential)

---

*INSTRUCTIONS for completion of the form are attached.
If space provided is insufficient, please use back of sheet.*

(A) Date_____
    Name_____Position_____Headquarters_____
    Age____Years with company____Years on present job____
                              (in present location)
    Educational background_____
                         (School, major subject, degree)
    Company job experience_____

    _____

    Company training_____
    State of health_____Are you transferable?_____
(If "conditional," check _____ and make comments on back)

(B) What elements of your present job do you think you
    do best?

(C) What do you regard as your greatest development
    needs?
        A. Technical (job knowledge)

        B. Management (administrative and supervisory
           skills)

(D) In what training and development activities do you
    think you might meet these needs?

there be some agreement concerning objectives, both short- and long-range, and plans to accomplish these objectives. Some companies include in these forms a redefinition of the responsibilities of the job (since the job may change slightly as conditions change), an agreement as to what evidence will be used to show progress or lack of it (in other words, deciding on the means of measurement that is mutually acceptable), and a statement of how much progress will be attempted to be made before the next meeting. Other companies suggest concentrating on accomplishments of the past and objectives for the future.

Note that all these procedures avoid one-sided judgments and the discussion of salaries. They avoid the causes of defensiveness—and stress *mutual* planning for improvement. They accentuate the positive and deemphasize the negative, which is probably why they are successful.

Other interviews. The interviews discussed so far have been either appraisal interviews or joint-planning interviews. But not all interviews are so easily classified. In the normal course of a day's work, a supervisor may have many discussions with his subordinates concerning work projects, their progress, or simply the details of operations—quality, safety, and many other matters. In the broad sense, these are interviews. And, because they avoid the major causes of defensiveness such as salary and the exercise of arbitrary judgment, they may be much more effective than the more formal interviews.

The formation of specific objectives, the progress toward these objectives, and the rewards for their accomplishment may be brought into these interviews in a natural way in direct connection with the discussion of operating details. The same may be true for the measurement and attainment of specific goals within these objectives. These are the interviews which provide the best coaching opportunities.

CASES

Coaching is a skill, and skills are learned by doing. Many of us can find opportunities in our own work situation to practice the principles of coaching. In the normal course of events, however, it may be years before he would experience all the standard situations. Also, a person who is really serious about wanting to become a better coach will want to practice so that, when he faces a situation in the workplace, he will be familiar with it having thought about and having dealt with a similar matter. For these reasons, the cases in this chapter are given so that the coach can:

1. Read and study them, listing the actions he would take if he were in a similar situation.
2. Read, study, and discuss them either informally or in a formal discussion group. The group as a whole can list possible courses of action for the coach.

*Many of us can find opportunities in our own
work situation to practice the principles of coaching.*

3. Meet with a discussion group where two people can play the roles of interviewer and
interviewee based on a case. A discussion by
the entire group can follow. The role playing
can be repeated by two or three teams, before
they go on to the next selected case.

Coaches can use their imagination to find other ways
of using these exercises to best fit their needs and

situation. It should be obvious that the more a person becomes involved, the more he will benefit. No solutions are provided to any of the cases because it is preferable that each coach work out his own solution.

Case 1

You are a general foreman, and you have a foreman, Bob, who consistently fails to face a certain problem. Although he organizes well and seldom overlooks a detail in planning or in follow-up, he lacks the forcefulness to insist that company rules be obeyed. One day you happen to overhear the following conversation between Bob and Charley, a furnace operator who works for him. You know that this is typical of the way Bob handles such situations.

BOB: How's your temperature running, Charley?
CHARLEY: O.K.
BOB: Are you checking the instrument to make sure it's running at about 1100 degrees?
CHARLEY: It's running at about 1100 degrees. The instrument controls the temperature. Don't worry about it. I know I'm supposed to check the instrument, but that's silly, and you know it. It never varies more than a few degrees. And, if it does, the instrument automatically takes

care of it. It's a waste of time for me to have to check it.

BOB: Well, you're probably right. It's only that if it ever should go haywire, we're supposed to know about it.

CHARLEY: Sure we are, but checking it every few minutes is stupid. Anyway, when you've been around here as long as I have, you know when things are wrong before the instruments do.

BOB: Well, I guess you're right. I don't know who wrote those rules anyway.

Case 2

A staff engineer working for you always fails to recognize the point at which a project no longer needs any work. It seems that once you put him on an assignment, he wants to stay on it forever. He is extremely thorough, but to him all details have the same value. You would like him to tell you when he thinks his progress is too slow or when a project is not worth continuing. You do not want to take the time to decide this yourself in every case.

Case 3

You are the supervisor of a research group in which there is a young research chemist. He is a bit cocky about the fact that he knows more chemistry than you and that his information and knowledge are more up to date than yours. He wants to do research but not in the area you want him to work in. He would prefer to work in related areas—close but not exactly on target. In fact, he has worked at home on papers which have been published, and he shows great promise. Now if only you could get him to work in the areas you designate.

Case 4

You have a technician in your laboratory whose work habits are inflexible. If he has already started a procedure when you supply him with new information, he will agree to evaluate it but you know he will continue along the path he started in spite of the new data. Sometimes this leads him to important discoveries, but usually it amounts to a great waste of time. You believe he will not develop if he does not adopt a more flexible attitude. In discussing routine job changes with him you are sometimes convinced that he wants to make the prescribed change, but on follow-up you find he does not make it. He likes you and you like him, but after talking to him about a change in the routine you usually feel as if you've been talking to yourself.

Case 5

You are a regional sales manager who supervises several local district sales managers. One of them is Joe Morton, a hard working, hard driving man who believes in the hard sell. He has the bad habit of harshly criticizing his route salesmen in front of each other. This has come to your attention from more than one source. You know that the turnover among his route salesmen is higher than average, and you feel that he is not reaching the full sales potential of his district. In your opinion, low morale among the salesmen is a major contributing factor. One day you attend a sales meeting that Joe is conducting with his route salesmen. When nearly all the salesmen have entered the room, but before the meeting starts, the following conversation transpires between Joe and Hank, one of the salesmen.

JOE: Did you put up that ten-case display at Carson's like I told you?

HANK: I didn't have enough supplies on my truck by the time I got there.

JOE: You mean you didn't do it?

HANK: I couldn't. I was nearly out of stock.

JOE *(in a loud voice)*: I specifically told you I wanted you to put up that display. Do you think I was just talking to hear myself talk? I really don't know about you. You don't rotate your stock, you don't put up a display, your records are ten days behind. How do you expect to sell anything? You've got to drive hard if you want to get anywhere in this business. I just don't know about you.

Case 6

You are a general foreman. Al Davenport, one of the men working for you, is the foreman of a packaging department that has several high-speed packaging machines. The department employs two setup men and twenty girls who are packers. Al has been in this department for 15 years, and many of his employees have been there nearly as long. They have an established routine which they are reluctant to change. You recognize that the department has been orderly and efficient in the past, but you can see that this efficiency is decreasing in relation to other departments where improvements are being made. You believe that the changes which will be required in the future are much more far-reaching than the changes of the past. You can see that the resistance of Davenport's department to making changes of any kind will ultimately be its downfall. It will also bring about your own downfall if you are not able to persuade them to stop resisting change.

Case 7

You are a plant engineer supervising a group of maintenance foremen, one of whom is Roy Hawkins. Roy is an excellent engineer. He seems to have a knack for going directly to the cause of mechanical problems. However, morale is low among Roy's mechanics. You are convinced that this is because of his manner. He seems to go out of his way to show his men that he has no respect for them. He seems to distrust them and they, in turn, distrust him. You feel that this one shortcoming may keep Roy from realizing his full potential. One day you accidentally hear the following conversation between Roy and Charley, one of his mechanics.

ROY: Charley, come into my office. I want to talk to you about your careless workmanship. I'm going to have to give you a day off.

CHARLEY: What job? What was wrong with it? Mac said it was O.K.

ROY: You know which job. Don't be coy with me. It was the pump job you "didn't" do yesterday.

CHARLEY: You'll never forget that little walk I took down to the cafeteria, will you?

ROY: Little walk! You were gone 45 minutes—and not once but several times.

CHARLEY: You've got a memory like an elephant. That was six months ago.

ROY: I've got a book on you! Do you want me to read you the dates and times?

CHARLEY: Ever since that one little incident, you've been carrying a grudge. All you want to do is get even with me.

ROY (*tapping his finger on Charley's shoulder*): Listen, I've been carrying you for as long as I'm going to. I've caught you reading comic books for the last time. And I've caught you goofing off in the corner for the last time. From now on you're going to pay. Now you're getting two days off!

Case 8

You are the administrator of a 500-bed hospital. One of your problems deals with an office manager who is reluctant to make decisions. Except for the easiest and most routine decisions, he puts them off as long as he can and then often gives only vague notions of what he thinks should be done. His subordinates know that getting him to make decisions is like pulling teeth. One of them said: "We usually try to figure it out for ourselves and then just go ahead." This man has many good qualities. He understands hospital office procedures exceptionally well, is meticulous about details, personally checks all work leaving the office, and rarely makes a mistake. It is your feeling, however, that he must learn to be more comfortable with his decision-making responsibilities if he is to make the contribution to the hospital that an office manager should.

Case 9

You are a sales manager whose major coaching problem is Karl Kalin, a salesman who does not follow through. Karl's strong points are his energy, his experience in other markets, and his sound and thorough planning. His weaknesses include a lack of firmness in dealing with people and the fact that his thorough planning is often not followed up by putting his plans into effect. You would like to strengthen his follow-up and feel that, if this could be done, he would be one of the outstanding salesmen in the company.

Case 10

You are a general foreman in the production department of a metalworking plant. You are concerned about Clarence Holden, one of the foremen under your supervision, because he sometimes does work which you feel he should delegate to others. In the last annual appraisal form, you rated Clarence as average in all respects except initiative, where you rated him above average but less than excellent. You noted that he has a good follow-through and sees ahead. You also noted that you feel he should delegate more of his work. The form also notes that he hopes to achieve promotion within the department.

Case 11

You are an office manager who supervises ten office workers: one black girl, seven white girls, and two white men. Your coaching problem involves Susan, the black girl. She has a reputation for being aggressive and for claiming discrimination when she does not get her own way. She is a good typist, knows the procedures, and is a conscientious worker. Because of her reputation, however, the other girls do not accept her. They sometimes accede to her wishes publicly in small matters. But they resent her privately and discuss their discontent among themselves. This works to everybody's disadvantage. Susan knows that she is resented and thinks it is because of her color. From your talks with the other office workers, you are convinced that it is not her color, but her behavior. You feel that, if you could persuade her to change her behavior, she would be accepted into the office group, and a serious morale problem would be solved, with improved effectiveness on the part of all concerned.

Case 12

You are a foreman supervising a workforce of twenty men, four of whom are black. You have been authorized to appoint an assistant foreman from your work group. The appointment is to be effective six weeks from the present date. The man most qualified for the job is Joe Jackson, who is black. Joe is well qualified in all respects but one. You are not sure that he is forceful enough to supervise both white and black workers. He knows the operation of the department well, his education is as good as your own, and he gets along well with his fellow operators. However, about a year ago, when he substituted as a utility man for a three-month period, you noticed that he had a certain hesitancy in dealing with the white operators. His duties as utility man included relieving the other operators on a schedule he prepared. Contractually, each operator was entitled to a relief period in the forenoon and one in the afternoon. Joe also handled operating emergencies as they arose. This gave him considerable leeway in adjusting his relief schedule, with the result that in some cases certain operators did not get the contractually required relief period. This resulted in bitterness, and sometimes in grievances. You have the feeling that Joe was afraid of being accused of favoring blacks and that he overcompensated by favoring the white operators. You wonder if he would do the same as assistant foreman and ultimately as foreman if he later takes your place. You wonder how you can use the next six weeks before the appointment to strengthen him on this point.

COACHING IN SPECIAL SITUATIONS

Coaching a person who does not respond to the same motivational incentives that you respond to can lead to frustration. Some men have experienced this in coaching women. For example, holding up the prospect of promotion to a young girl whose only reason for working is to earn enough money for a trousseau causes the supervisor not only to fail but to look ridiculous. In addition, not all men respond in the same way to the prospect of a $25-a-month raise, an added status symbol, or an impressive title. When a coach encounters someone who does not respond to such incentives in the traditional way, he may be at a loss to know how to proceed. The feeling is much like that of the automobile driver whose car suddenly starts skidding on a slippery pavement. Steering wheel, brakes, accelerator—not one of these works the way the driver is accustomed to. He has no control. He is helpless.

A current example of a supervisor trying to coach a person who does not respond in the traditional ways is that of a white supervisor coaching a black employee. If the black employee is from a middle- or upper-class culture, the supervisor may encounter no more than the usual difficulty. But if the black worker is from a ghetto culture and the white supervisor is not, they may not only speak different languages but they may respond differently to the same stimuli. Hence, the supervisor may be rewarding the worker when he thinks he is punishing him, and vice versa. For example, a disciplinary layoff without pay is regarded by most people as a punishment. However, a man from the ghetto may regard the layoff as a holiday. When he turns down a job opportunity that the white supervisor thinks is highly desirable, this may reveal a difference in values based on cultural background. This was true in the case of Henry Ellis.

Henry was a white foreman supervising a mixed group of industrial workers, one of whom was Roy Simmons, a black employee from the ghetto. One of Henry's problems was that Roy was a chronic absentee. Henry said to Roy, "Look, this is an expanding company with good jobs opening up all over, and they're open to blacks. But I can't recommend you for one of these jobs if I can't count on your being here five days out of five. I can't recommend that they give you more responsibility when you aren't handling the respon-

142

sibility you've got now. This company is crying for men who can take responsibility. You could be a member of management. This is your golden opportunity." But Roy's answer was, "Golden opportunity? I don't see any golden opportunity in it. I've heard that story before."

Roy's reaction showed Henry that Roy was not accepting his words at face value. Roy did not see an opportunity where Henry saw it, and he did not respond to the situation in the way Henry would have responded.

What can the white supervisor do in this situation? There is really no answer, except the one the individuals work out for themselves. Henry Ellis could seek the advice of a black friend, especially one who is a supervisor himself. He might try to find out whether Roy Simmons has set any personal goals for himself and, if so, what they are. If he has not set any, Henry might try to help him set some by surveying all possible opportunities. Once Roy's goals have been established, Henry could make a few suggestions about training, self-discipline, and housekeeping. Joe Jackson's supervisor (see Case 12) might give Joe an opportunity to practice supervising in a limited way during his six-week training period. He could try to build up Joe's confidence in his ability to supervise. He might call the other men together and, in Joe's presence, tell them the extent to which Joe is being given authority and explain the reasons for it. He might ask for their cooperation.

The young girl, mentioned earlier, who is working to finance a trousseau might respond to a pay raise even though she would not respond to the possibility of a promotion. Job satisfaction could be a motivator. Prestige, work surroundings, time off, nature of duties—these factors may affect her quite differently from the way they would another person. A coach's good listening skills are required to find out.

Surely the white coach of a black employee such as Roy Simmons will need to depend even more than usual on his listening skills. He will need to heighten his sensitivity to the needs, desires, and drives of the employee. He will need to depend even more than usual on joint planning, especially in setting objectives. He will need to intensify his efforts to help, and to restrict if not completely eliminate his efforts to advise. All his powers of observation will be needed to help him detect patterns of action and reaction. When he has established a stable relationship—that is, a relationship in which reactions can be predicted with some accuracy—then he may consider ways of influencing the employee's habitual behavior on the job through the use of one or more of the six basic coaching strategies.

9

Dealing with Difficult Employee Behavior

THE supervisor or other leader often has to cope with difficult behavior in the people he supervises. The vast majority of people can be expected to conform to normally accepted standards of behavior. Sooner or later, though, most leaders come in contact with individuals who insist upon being different— and difficult. The problem is compounded for the supervisor of these people. Not only is he forced to deal with them, but they are on his team. He must

145

try to develop them to their maximum potential or deny that employee development is part of his job as a supervisor.

The reasons for a person's behaving in a particular way may be as difficult to identify as the causes of the common cold. These reasons may be countless and next to impossible to determine. But this need not cause the coach to stop trying to influence employee behavior, provided of course that in doing so he is trying to help the person and increase his overall contribution to the organization. As a supervisor, he must never forget his dual obligation to the individual and to the organization. Given the necessary insight, the required coaching skill, and the time to give the matter the attention it deserves, he can develop a positive program of improvement.

Every coaching action takes place in a specific climate and each involves at least two unique individuals. Therefore, a possible solution or technique that appeals to one coach will not necessarily appeal to another. This chapter provides an opportunity for deeper insight into coaching problems through consideration of several difficult behavior patterns. These are patterns that coaches have had to deal with in the past and that coaches of the present are still dealing with. No "cures" are prescribed, for to attempt to reduce human behavior to formulas is to fail. Some possible courses of action that have

*Every coaching action takes place in a specific climate,
and each involves at least two unique individuals.*

been suggested by various coaches are listed. Each
suggestion or comment grew out of a specific situation. It should be apparent that as situations vary so
will workable solutions.

Also, the checklists are not intended to be complete. They are offered as guides to help the coach
choose possible solutions that suit his style. The
statements for evaluation may be true or false, almost
true, or almost false. They reflect attitudes or opinions concerning ways to handle the designated

147

behavior. They do not necessarily reflect the best attitudes or even recommended attitudes, but they are typical of some supervisors.

A thoughtful study of these employee behavior patterns with the accompanying statements and the suggestions and comments will help the serious coach to discover his own attitudes, to focus more sharply on his own preferred courses of action, and to understand more clearly the reasons for his preferences.

FAILURE TO SHOW INITIATIVE

Statement for evaluation: "I let my employees know that they don't get far with me if they don't show initiative. The best way to encourage initiative is to let them know you expect it and then prod them about it every couple of weeks."

Some possible courses of action:
Set some goals.
Assign areas of work.
Use group discussion.
Encourage competition by comparisons. Post comparative performance records on bulletin boards.
Enforce high standards.
Encourage ideas.
Create competition.
Recognize achievement.

Provide occasions for the use of initiative.
Give consistent encouragement.
Build up employee's good points.

DULL BEHAVIOR

Statement for evaluation: "The reason people are dull is that they are too lazy to think, and the more patient you are with them, the lazier they become."

Some possible courses of action:
Change routine.
Set an example.
Set goals.
Supervise more closely.
Set time schedules.
Line up interests with work.

COVERT OPPOSITION TO AUTHORITY

Statement for evaluation: "The best way to overcome opposition is to beat your enemies at their own game and prove your right to leadership."

Some possible courses of action:
Force the opposition out into the open.
Confront the employee and challenge him to voice his opposition.
Ask for his advice.

OVERT OPPOSITION TO AUTHORITY

Statement for evaluation: "A real supervisor never faces open opposition, because people know they cannot succeed against him."

Some possible courses of action:
Praise the employee for cooperation.
Counsel the employee on his goals.
Reprimand the employee.

DISHONESTY

Statement for evaluation: "It is hard to determine the moral quality of a dishonest act, and such decisions are best left to the courts."

Some possible courses of action:
Search for the cause.
Show the employee how it hurts his chances.
Fire a dishonest person immediately.
Don't judge lest you be judged.
Point out that dishonesty does not pay.

LACK OF FOLLOW-THROUGH

Statement for evaluation: "When an employee starts a project, don't let him drop it. When he learns you won't stand for lack of perseverance, he will know he has to finish what he starts."

Some possible courses of action:
Check employee's progress.
Set deadlines.
Needle the employee.
Coach him on follow-up.
Help him adopt a system.
Increase your own follow-up.
Develop his pride in the job.
Develop a system of rewards and punishments.
Require a written statement of his plans.

IRRESPONSIBILITY

Statement for evaluation: "The surest way to cure a man of irresponsibility is to let him suffer the full penalty. Experience is the best teacher."

Some possible courses of action:
Give the employee specific responsibilities and encourage action.
Find the cause.
Insist on high quality work.
Measure efficiency.
Praise or punish.
Motivate the employee by stressing the importance of his job.

UNRELIABILITY

Statement for evaluation: "Attempts to reform unreliable employees are commendable, but keeping

151

an unreliable employee on the payroll may cause a supervisor to lose his own job."

Some possible courses of action:
Emphasize the importance of dependability.
Explain to the employee why you must depend on him.
Build up his interest in the job.

PREJUDICE

Statement for evaluation: "A supervisor who wastes time with a prejudiced man loses standing. Employees will laugh at any boss who tries to convince a fool."

Some possible courses of action:
Expose the employee to the facts.
Find the emotional cause of the prejudice and concentrate on it.
Work around his prejudices.

DISLOYALTY

Statement for evaluation: "A man whose loyalty to me is such that he openly criticizes my conduct is not a suitable member of my organization."

Some possible courses of action:
Improve the employee's understanding of the entire problem.

Inform him of policy.
Improve communication.
Earn his loyalty.

AGITATION OF OTHER EMPLOYEES

Statement for evaluation: "The way to deal with an agitator is to keep him so busy he won't have time to stir up trouble."

Some possible courses of action:
Find a way to use the employee's excess energy.
Assign him responsibility.
Isolate him.
Publish the truth.
Give him attention.
Keep him working.
Give him a constructive cause to work for.

DISCOURTESY

Statement for evaluation: "No man is discourteous by accident. Therefore nothing is gained by overlooking the first offense."

Some possible courses of action:
Find the cause.
Have a private interview with the employee and face the issue.
Ignore it. It may be that the employee is having a bad day.

Stubbornness

Statement for evaluation: "Never argue with a stubborn man. Action is the only language he understands."

Some possible courses of action:
Consult with the employee.
Tell him why something must be done.
Work around him.
Force compliance.

Chronic Complaints About Wages

Statement for evaluation: "When a man chronically complains about his salary, I study the job and find some way to rearrange the work so as to reduce the salary rather than raise it. My employees know this and have stopped bringing me complaints."

Some possible courses of action:
Get the facts.
Study the job with an open mind.
Be fair.
Find the cause of discontent.

Cowardice

Statement for evaluation: "If an employee doesn't have enough courage to withstand intimidation from

154

other employees, he is not the type of person that I care to keep."

Some possible courses of action:
Make the employee angry.
Build his self-confidence by giving him day-to-day coaching; praising him when he deserves it; assigning him a special project; assigning him responsibility; insuring that he will not fail.
Improve his technical competence.
Reassure him.

SULKING

Statement for evaluation: "A man is sullen only when he dares to be. Sullenness doesn't appear when competent supervisors are in charge."

Some possible courses of action:
Find the cause and deal with it.
Ignore it. Everybody has a bad day once in a while.
Try to bring it out into the open.

The foregoing provides material for thought and for discussion in formal or informal training sessions. In order to gain the maximum benefit from these exercises, the coach should look for opportunities to

Figure 4. Form for checklist and follow-up.

Coaching Checklist	
Name _____	
Behavior pattern to encourage	Behavior pattern to improve
Possible action 1. 2. 3. 4.	Possible action 1. 2. 3. 4.
Most suitable action	Most suitable action
Dates of coaching action 1. 2. 3.	Dates of coaching action 1. 2. 3.

apply them on the job. The on-the-job application can follow the same pattern as the exercises. First, identify the behavior; second, make a list of the possible courses of action; third, select the best alternatives; and fourth, apply the corrective action. A convenient form for use as a checklist and for follow-up is shown in Figure 4.

10

A Final Review of Coaching

ON-THE-JOB coaching is usually performed in a supervisor-subordinate situation. The relationship between supervisor and subordinate provides the climate for coaching. The coach can improve communication and encourage freedom of action by de-emphasizing the verticalness of the relationship and emphasizing the horizontalness. Inasmuch as verticalness inhibits both communication and action, playing it down removes the inhibition, thereby allowing learning to take place.

Adult learning is defined as a modification of behavior through experience. The goal of the coach is to change habitual on-the-job behavior. The change is brought about in complex ways. However, it is sometimes useful to simplify the process for easy understanding. One such effort is represented by the four-step learning model. It presents the learning process as (1) recognizing a lack or a need, (2) identifying what is needed, (3) wanting what is needed, and (4) taking steps to acquire it. The coach's problem is to make sure that the learner experiences the four steps of the process.

The process is the subject of some misconceptions which may limit the effectiveness of the coach. "Experience is the best teacher" is one. The successful coach knows that not all people learn from their experiences. The lives of some people are simply repetitions of past patterns, revealing that little is new and nothing is learned. Experience teaches only when the mind is prepared to detect and analyze new patterns. Similarly, "You can't teach an old dog new tricks" is true only if the old dog has closed his mind to the possibility of change. Given the proper attitude, age does not preclude learning. Another misconception is attached to "Practice makes perfect." A successful coach knows that practice improves performance only when new and better patterns are being practiced. And it is the coach's job to recommend these better patterns. Theoretically, a person could find the patterns himself, given enough time. But if the coach really knows superior methods, he can save the learner time and effort by providing him with them so that the methods practiced do indeed lead to improved performance.

Improved performance is the objective of adult learning, which is different from the learning of children. First, it is powerfully influenced by past experience. The child has had experience, but the adult has had more. Second, adult learning is influenced by how the adult sees himself. The child sees himself as dependent; the adult sees himself as independent. To the coach, these differences mean that he may be able to use the adult's experience to aid the learning and that choices should be left for the independent adult to make.

Adult learning situations should be nonthreatening. Coaching should be applied in small steps, as in programmed instruction, so that the learner does not opt out. Adults have images of themselves which they need to have polished and improved. They will more readily learn those things that they believe will enhance their images, making them greater in the eyes of those they wish to please.

Any on-the-job coaching device can be expected to succeed if it sticks to the fundamentals of adult learning and if it fits the situation. Some commonly used coaching devices are job rotation, assignment of special projects, membership in professional societies, enrollment in formal classes, temporary vacation replacement, representation of superiors at meetings, and participation in committee assignments. However, it is generally conceded that the most effective way to influence on-the-job behavior is through day-to-day coaching.

Six major strategies of day-to-day coaching have been identified: (1) change the environment, (2) reward and punish, (3) prescribe and supervise key points, (4) make joint plans, (5) control the rate at which the employee takes on responsibility, and (6) coach the extremes. Changing the environment is an effective strategy because any intelligent organism adjusts to a changed environment almost automatically. An adult will adjust in ways he thinks are consistent with the self-image he wishes to present to himself and others, so changing the environment will bring adjustments in behavior. Related to this idea is the strategy of rewarding desired behavior and punishing undesired behavior. Since behavior is influenced by these rewards and punishments, a change in the system of administering them may cause a change in behavior. Supervising key points is a matter of focusing on selected aspects of behavior in an effort to establish new patterns.

The rationale for the strategy of joint planning lies in the idea that a person will try harder to ac-

If he deliberately plans his daily efforts
to change the habitual behavior of his subordinates,
he is a coach.

complish goals if he has set them for himself, or has helped to set them, than if they were set by others. With joint planning, the coach involves the learner not only in the process of setting objectives but also in making plans to reach the objectives. Controlling the rate at which an employee takes on responsibility can be useful when the person being coached is expected to increase his rate of growth or when he is

162

learning a new job. Responsibility and accountability are assigned in measured amounts which are supposed to challenge the person to extend himself. But he is not supposed to be defeated by the challenge. Coaching the extremes is a strategy of concentrating simultaneously on the person's strongest points and his weakest points, with emphasis on the former.

A supervisor is not only a supervisor. He is a teacher. Even if he does nothing to promote himself in his role as a teacher, his subordinates still learn from his example. If he deliberately plans his daily efforts to change the habitual behavior of his subordinates, he is a coach.

Annotated Bibliography

Banaka, William H. "Invention: A Key to Effective Coaching." *Training and Development Journal* 21 (November 1967): 44–52. This article describes a coaching course used by Tektronix. It centers on the use of performance indicators in coaching interviews.

Black, James Menzies. "How to Coach a Winning Management Team." in *How to Grow in Management*. Englewood Cliffs, N.J.: Prentice-Hall, Inc., 1957, pp. 57–72. This book contains general coaching advice for executives. It includes a ten-question multiple-choice quiz for evaluating coachmanship.

Cady, Edwin Laird. *Developing Executive Capacity*. Englewood Cliffs, N.J.: Prentice-Hall, Inc., 1958. This is a book on do-it-yourself executive development. It is aimed at helping a person become an executive and then helping an executive become more effective.

Coffin, Tris. "Help Yourself to Executive Skill." *Nation's Business* 46 (September 1958): 68–72. This article reports on research at General Electric conducted by Moorhead Wright. The research concluded that a man's development is 90 percent the result of his experience in his day-to-day work. Because of this research, the responsibility for an executive's development rests on the executive himself and on his supervisor as well. Ten basic principles to guide a company in developing its people are introduced.

"Executive Coaching Catches On." *Business Week* (March 9, 1967): 61–72. Engineers are hard to get and harder to hold. And, according to this article, they should get special treatment. A brief description of the coaching process is supplied.

Gemmill, Gary. "Managing Upward Communication." *Personnel Journal* 49 (February 1970) : 107–110. This article gives insight into the inhibitions that limit frank communication between supervisor and subordinate. These inhibitions discourage trust and must be overcome by coaching.

Goodacre, Daniel M., III. "Changing On-the-Job Behavior: How and Where to Start." *Personnel* 37 (May–June 1960): 58–62. A nonthreatening climate for growth is an essential condition for behavior change. This article describes sensitivity training and suggests that its principles can be applied to on-the-job situations.

Gould, M. I. "Counseling for Self-Development." *Personnel Journal* 49 (March 1970): 226–234. A training director describes how personal interviews are used to enhance goal setting, self-appraisal, establishment of plans of action, and the management of behavioral change. Examples from typical interviews are included.

————. "Improving Coaching Skills." *Personnel Administration* 27 (January–February 1964): 28–33. Research shows that people want to be coached. Based on this premise, this article presents specific courses of action to improve managers' coaching techniques.

Kellogg, Marion S. "The Coaching Appraisal: A Tool for Better Delegation." *Supervisory Management* 10 (September 1965): 4–7. This article deals with the mechanics of preparing a document that records the results of a coaching appraisal. The appraisal is shown to have three parts: (1) ability to do the job, (2) factors over which the employee has no control but which affect performance, and (3) the manager's own ability to help the employee.

Kopf, Richard G. "Coaching and Counseling Managers." *Journal of the American Society of Training Directors* 15 (March 1961): 40–53. Counseling is the main concern of this article. To a large extent, each of us sets his own standards, judges his own performance, and determines his own requirements for improvement. The article views the coach as directive, aiming at developing skills, whereas the counselor is viewed as nondirective, aiming at helping the man to develop himself.

Levinson, Harry. "A Psychologist Looks at Executive Development." *Harvard Business Review* 40 (September–October 1962): 69–75. This article says that coaching in most U.S. businesses falls short of the mark because (1) there is not enough time, (2) mistakes are not allowed, (3) personal dependency needs are rejected, (4) rivalry is repressed, and (5) the coaching relationship is unexamined.

Likert, Rensis. "Motivational Approach to Management Development." *Harvard Business Review* 37 (July–

August 1959): 75–82. Coaching in appraisal interviews is stressed. The author discusses joint-planning sessions in which standards of performance quantity and quality are agreed upon. He then reviews certain behavioral research dealing with the social climate in which coaching is performed.

Mace, Myles L., and Walter R. Mahler. "On-the-Job Coaching." In *Developing Executive Skills,* H. F. Merrill and E. Marting, eds., AMA, 1958, pp. 99–110. Many people do not know what their bosses expect of them. Coaching is so informal and haphazard at times that people do not even know when they are being coached. Since on-the-job learning is largely the responsibility of the manager, this book offers advice on how managers can become more effective coaches. The book also discusses delegation, counseling, teamwork, and mutual confidence, and it deals with determining standards that are to be set.

Miljus, Robert C. "Effective Leadership and the Motivation of Human Resources." *Personnel Journal* 49 (January 1970): 36–40. This article contains eight practical suggestions on how to create an environment that would improve on-the-job effectiveness.

Miller, Norman R. "Career Guidance—A Means of Tapping Hidden Potential." *Personnel* 41 (July–August 1964): 36–42. The viewpoint expressed in this article is that a man's career can best be guided by someone other than his supervisor.

Pelfry, R. H. "What a Manager Can Learn from Pro Football." *Supervisory Management* 11 (December 1966): 5–7. A former professional football player points out some coaching principles that seem to work as well in the office as they do on the football field.

Pettit, Albert E. "Mid-management Does the Training." *Journal of the American Society of Training Directors*

COACHING, LEARNING, AND ACTION

14 (January 1960): 24–30. According to this article, the training function, including coaching, belongs to a man's immediate supervisor. A specific effort on the part of one company to strengthen on-the-job training is described.

Read, William M. "Common Sense About Coaching." *Supervisory Management* 11 (March 1966): 16–19. This article emphasizes the need for a supervisor to coach. It states that the coaching responsibility is often avoided, and it offers some general ideas about coaching.

————. "Supervision Is Coaching." *Supervisory Management* 5 (November 1960): 33–38. This article first emphasizes that the supervisor is a coach and then offers positive ideas on how he should approach coaching.

"Reality Instead of Role-Play." *Sales Management* 98, Part Two (March 15, 1967) : 156–160. Team conferences in cars after actual sales calls provide effective coaching sessions. This article describes this team coaching technique used by Flexnit Company, Inc.

Richards, John C. "Building Coaching into the Manager's Job." *Personnel* 38 (May–June 1961): 43–51. An important part of a manager's job is to develop his subordinates' skills and to convey his own managerial skills to his subordinates. A logical and systematic approach to the problem is suggested.

Rowland, Virgil K. *Improving Managerial Performance.* New York: Harper & Brothers, 1958, pp. 110–116. The section entitled "The Role of the Coach" deals with the problems of a staff man, called a coach, who attends a performance appraisal interview with a manager.

Singer, Edwin. "Overlooking Coaching." *Personnel Management* 1 (November 1969): 44–48. Many bosses leave their lower-level managers to sink or swim instead of helping them improve their performance by on-the-job coaching. The importance of coaching and the way it can be

approached are described in this article. Five characteristics of a good coach are also given.

Thomas, David. "The Case for Planned Development."
Personnel 38 (March–April 1961): 8–17. This article discusses the supervisor's role as coach and his responsibility
for developing and encouraging his subordinates. It emphasizes goal setting and introduces the idea that improving operations may be more profitable than improving individuals.

Weatherbee, Harvard Y. "Steering Marginal Performers to
Solid Ground." *Personnel* 46 (July–August 1969): 34–43.
The coaching procedure described in this article is analysis, action determination, and implementation. Analysis
includes identifying the marginal performer and then
learning why he is marginal. Action determination includes deciding whether to fire him, transfer him, or try
to improve his performance through coaching. Implementation relies heavily on the use of formal appraisals
and the measurement of results.

Wikstron, Walter S. *Developing Managerial Competence.*
New York: National Industrial Conference Board, 1964,
pp. 56–59. This brief section of the book contains a
developmental planning checklist which is used by The
Boeing Company for coaching supervisors.

Wright, Moorhead. "Individual Growth: The Basic Principles." *Personnel* 37 (September–October 1960): 8–18.
This article lists and discusses ten basic principles of on-
the-job coaching. They evolved from research done by
the author at General Electric. The responsibility of the
line manager for development of his subordinates is emphasized.